# DR. WIDOW

# DR. WIDOW

## A BOOK OF TWO JOURNEYS…..
## AND HOW TO SURVIVE THEM BOTH

## ZARINA GARRISON

**To order additional copies of this book, contact:**
Xlibris
1-888-795-4274
www.Xlibris.com
Orders@Xlibris.com
806272

# CONTENTS

# DEDICATION

This book is dedicated firstly to my children, who show me the everyday magic that big people take for granted. They make me feel as though we can do anything as a family, including surviving Mommy's doctoral program and Daddy's untimely death. With all the love I have left to give in this life, I will love these two always. For that matter, Daddy would be so proud of the people you are becoming, and it is my humble honor to share his memory with you in this way.

Secondly, this book is dedicated to all of the widows and widowers out there that (unfortunately) are created every day. You are my people, and I wouldn't be healing (or even functioning) without my fellow widows' support and guidance along the way. This book is our book; this knowledge is ours to share so that others in the world who have never been through losing a spouse/partner can better understand what we see, feel, and do.

Lastly, this book is dedicated to the friends and family who continually show love and support of the life I lead with my kids and my aspirations to write. My parents especially have provided me clarity and strength during the darkest periods of my life. This book would not have been possible without them.

# ACKNOWLEDGMENTS

THERE WAS NO ONE SINGULAR person to acknowledge that greatly influenced this book, save of course, my late husband. He, by far, was the better half in the relationship, and his death at the age of thirty-two shook me to my core. Even in passing, he inspires me to do better, to be better, and to help others do the same. True to the title, I wouldn't be a doctor *or* widow without the love and support of this man.

That being said, I must also acknowledge the guidance and feedback provided by my publisher, Xlibris, who helped make a lifelong dream of becoming an author a reality. This book is part of a genre I never thought I would contribute to, and they helped me navigate the unfamiliar to complete this book.

I also choose to acknowledge the widow and doctoral support groups I have participated in since 2016. These organizations are populated by the most inspiring, strong, and resilient people I have ever had the privilege of meeting. To be considered one of their ranks is a gift. Thank you all for sharing your experiences with me and for helping me appreciate my new life status with multiple perspectives.

# INTRODUCTION

LET ME BE PERFECTLY CLEAR when I make the following statement: being a widow sucks! Any way you dissect the components of widowhood, it all ends up a hot mess of refuse and hurt. It can come at you sideways and unexpectedly; it can be preordained yet still powerfully painful; it can even occur when grieving the loss of an ex-spouse. In my case, I kissed my husband goodbye for work one fine Friday morning, and that was the last I saw him. His car accident shattered my understanding of the universe and made time stand still. The man I had loved for more than half of my life, and whom I had vowed to spend eternity with, was gone. How could I survive when he did not? How could I carry on when he could not? What was I going to do with my life now? All these questions and approximately a million more were circling my mind's eye like vultures before the feast. My sanity, my happiness, I daresay my will to live was challenged on the day of December 16, 2016. But like many widows/ widowers, life has a way of forcing us to carry on. I became a widow at age thirty, which meant I also became a single mother (something I also did not plan ever to be). On December 17, 2016, I found myself thirty, single, raising an eighteen-month-old and a three-year-old—both of whom who were grieving the loss of Daddy and wondering why he wouldn't be there for Christmas. I can honestly say that my two children have been and will forever remain my guardian angels. My will to love and nurture them almost immediately overpowered my need to curl up and die in a dark corner. Without them, my journey, and this book, would be very different indeed.

Oh, and did I mention I was a doctoral student at the time? I had been attending school for two years when the accident occurred. I was at a stage in my academic program where slowing down momentum would have prevented me from graduating altogether. I had begun the doctoral journey both to advance myself professionally and to appease the part of my brain that has always wanted to be a doctor, but was that enough to survive the road ahead? When the weight of the world fell squarely on my shoulders, and only my shoulders now, how could I be both mother and student, widow and scholar? I did not have an answer to these questions as I began to tread the uncharted waters of my new social status: #widow. I remember collapsing into my sister's arms and telling her, "I don't know how to do this."

Rewind time a bit, and you will have seen me outwit, outthink, and outsmart any test in my childhood. There was no subject too hard, and no assignment too difficult. But this wasn't an academic issue; this was an issue most adults don't endure until retirement. And here I was, unprepared for the test before me.

For all of the questions I did not have an answer for, there were two questions whose answers seemed clear: "Do I need to heal from this hurt?" and "Do I need to finish my degree?" I knew in my soul that the answer to these questions was a resounding *yes*. The real issue, as with most things in life, is *how* could I heal and *how* could I finish my degree? Therein lies the need for this book. There is a great deal of support groups, books, social media groups, and organizations aimed at helping widows. However, the media and literature seem to be sparse on what to do when you find yourself both widowed and pursuing a PhD level degree. Since I experienced both simultaneously, it is difficult for me to disseminate the heartache and challenges that each journey can impose individually. I found myself seeking resources for widows that did not address the stress of homework assignments and seeking support from doctoral resources who did not understand trying to clear one's mind while grieving. Frankly, I think that if you find yourself in the position I was in, burying your head in the sand for an undetermined amount of time is a wholly acceptable and valid method to cope. But realistically, isolation is not healthy, atrophy of the mind is damaging, and relentless sojourning for answers is the plight of anyone who desires to pursue a terminal degree. I suppose you could say that I wrote this book to help fellow Dr. Widows (or aspiring Dr. Widows) survive the dual journey they are on by sharing the lessons I have learned along the way.

While this book addresses the rather unique identity of Dr. Widow, I'd like to think that the lessons learned about grit and perseverance are relevant to anybody who has experienced loss or who is studying at the collegiate level. Sometimes, the best life lessons can come from places we did not expect, so I encourage anyone reading this book, regardless of their state of being, to be receptive to the lessons it provides. I thought once that writing a book and baring my soul on the page would be difficult, embarrassing, and foreign. But even as I write this introduction, I feel a sense of calm knowing that I am sharing all of me for the benefit of others. Anyone who has been hurt, or is hurting, should know that I am a comrade-in-arms; anybody who has spent sleepless nights studying or questioned their abilities understand that I have felt that inner torment as well (because the doctoral journey is a gauntlet in its own right).

This book is many things—a diary, a novel, a self-help book, a how-to guide—but for me, it is a type of support I didn't know I needed. There was a cathartic pleasure gained in assembling and reassembling the memories I have experienced over the past three years. It has become the best therapy I never paid for, to use one of my mother's idioms. The book is organized using the five stages of grief model developed by another doctor, Dr. Kubler-Ross. Her work in loss and grieving was something that I had researched previously as a foster parent. Little did I know how invaluable that knowledge would be for my own healing in the future.

As part of my own grief therapy, I wrote haikus during each stage of grief; some of which are in each chapter. Each of the five stages of grief (denial, anger, bargaining, depression, and acceptance) will include stories of my life (all of which are true), major elements of the doctoral journey, and how I personally overcame the hurdles of each stage. The book is also riddled with my own quirky sense of humor throughout (1) because it is one my coping mechanisms and (2) because if you are not laughing, you are crying (especially for widows). The book ends with where I go from here (because the dual journey of Dr. Widow is not over), and I hope you too find a sense of moving forward.

From the bottom of my heart (all the way to the top), thank you.

# CHAPTER 1

# Denial of Widows

Waiting to find you
Was two days/eternity:
Fear, hate, deny, sad

I'm a single mom
I did everything right, but
I'm a single mom

We talked about death.
You said I could remarry . . .
Jason Momoa . . .

## The Accident

IT WAS THE COLDEST DAY so far that winter in our little corner of Nebraska. At 5:00 p.m., it was already black as night outside. I was humming whatever Christmas tune was on the radio while cooking my husband's favorite meal. It had been his thirty-second birthday just three days before, but we had been so busy planning my daughter's third birthday (she was born three days after Daddy) that we really hadn't done anything to celebrate his day. In point of fact, I had planned to spoil him rotten the whole weekend—favorite foods, TV shows, foot rub, the whole nine yards. But as five-thirty rolled around, I began to worry a bit for my husband. Not mortal peril worry, but worry like "I hope he is not lost." My husband had just started a new position in the Midwest after spending his entire life previously in his hometown of Tucson, Arizona. I remember even on the best days in Arizona that my husband had the innate ability to get lost in a closet, let alone a whole new town. So I worried a little more. I called his phone, no answer.

At about six-thirty, the nail biting had begun, the dinner was burnt and cooling off, and I had phoned my father to help me look for Samuel. My dad, who will forever be my superhero, knew I had two small babies at home and couldn't safely cruise around town looking for my husband. He coordinated efforts between himself and my visiting relatives to comb the streets. Unfortunately, by midnight, we had still not found, seen, or heard from Samuel. I tracked his phone—wasn't registering. I called his work—no answer. We retraced his path home from work and any variation in between—no luck.

At 1:00 a.m., I am gutted to call my in-laws and have the phone conversation with them that their only child, their baby boy, was missing. I tried telling them not to worry because we did not know for sure where he was or how he was doing. But in my heart, the little black void had already begun to grow. At two, my sister in Arizona had texted me a picture of a car accident covered on the local news. The picture was dark, blurry, and the car was aflame. My dad was in denial, saying that the car didn't even look like Samuel's. But I had a gut feeling that he was putting on a game face to keep me strong and not lose hope. I, however, was more concerned with how much it did look like Samuel's Corolla, even down to the missing rear hubcap on the driver's side. I remember fighting the urge to accept the potential reality that Samuel had died—the denial had already started to set in.

Saturday morning, the local sheriff's department had come to my home to ask me a few questions since we reported Samuel as a missing person the night before. They wanted to know details about him, his car, and wanted to get a copy of his dental records. The car accident I saw in the photo was actually one of three fatal accidents that night due to black ice, and additionally, there were a great number of missing-person reports. They wanted dental records to rule out Samuel from any of these situations. They said it calmly and even tried to smirk like we were all going to laugh about this when he turned up, regaling us with a story of temporary amnesia and wandering the streets. But I was not buying it.

At about 4:00 a.m., before the sheriff deputies had arrived, I felt Samuel hold me in his arms before floating away. Mind you, I had historically been skeptical about ghosts and the manifestation of spirits—another denial I suppose. It was now the weekend, so all I could do was provide the deputies with Samuel's old dental office contact in Arizona and hope against hope that they answer their phones on the weekends. Turns out they didn't.

I spent the rest of the weekend in a fog. I did not eat much, did not sleep much. I cooked food for my kids and cuddled with them a lot. My little sister and her husband, part of the street-combing crew, hugged me and were solemn. My husband and I were high school sweethearts. We had spent over fifteen years together. He was more brother than brother-in-law to my sisters. They were worried and hurting too, but what shut them down more was not knowing what to do for me—the would-be widow.

On Monday, December 19, 2016, the sheriff's deputies knocked on my door again. This time, it was to confirm that the body identified in the burning car was of my husband, Samuel Garrison, confirmed by dental records. Apparently, he was coming home from work and hit a particularly large patch of black ice, causing him to skid across the oncoming lane of traffic and wrap around a tree. He died on impact, and the car caught fire for about fifteen minutes before it could be extinguished.

I heard these words exiting the mouths of the deputies. I saw their lips hesitant to bring such bad tidings, especially during the holidays. I watched their brows furrow, fighting back their own tears at watching a young mother and her two kids try to play underfoot. I heard the utter silence from my sister and brother-in-law who had followed the deputies into the house from outside, having gone out one last time searching for Samuel. But mostly, I remember hearing a high-pitch ringing in my ears and an inner voice shouting, "How the fuck could this be happening?"

Denial. I remained calm and level-headed with the officers. I thanked them for their time and told them, choking back hot tears, "When I saw the picture, I sort of figured."

But I didn't figure. Sure, the logical lizard-brain side of me knew what I saw, connected all the dots. But the side of me that was ripping to shreds inside never ever, ever, ever, ever saw this coming. We were young, healthy, just starting new careers and academic journeys, and we had a beautiful family to boot. There was no way; it was not possible.

Immediately after closing the front door, my sister instinctually caught me as I crumbled into her arms, wailing into her shoulder so as to not disturb my babies. My brother-in-law hugged me and cried—the one and only time I had ever seen him shed a tear.

I excused myself and went to my room for a minute. I began having a conversation with myself out loud about what was going on and what I needed to do when the reality was, I didn't really have a clue what to do nor did anyone else in my family. With the exception of my ninety-year-old grandmother, I was the first widow in the family.

That night, I spent the rest of the evening and into the early morning hours the next day laughing in bed. *It is all a mistake—Samuel will turn up tomorrow. He is just lost.* My brain even began to jump to more outlandish conclusions like he was now in witness protection and he had to leave me and the kids behind for our protection. Or he was a spy, and the body in the car was to fake his own death! I kept telling myself like a mantra, "This didn't happen. This is not me. I will not be a single mom. I will not go through life alone. This didn't happen. I am *not* a widow."

---

I think that it is very easy to slip into the denial stage of grief. Not wanting to lose a loved one is natural, and trying to rationalize them as being alive is also part of our DNA. I could almost forgive myself for this initial denial. But it took me a long time to figure out why I was continuing to deny his death in public, and even though I was the one doing the denying, it angered me. *Why are you lying?* I thought to myself. *Why hide away from your new reality?*

Then it occurred to me that two fundamental things were happening when I denied my widowhood in public: (1) there is an unavoidable stigma people impose on you once they find out you are widowed (which made me feel very insecure), and (2) me saying it out loud was one step closer to accepting his loss, and I simply wasn't at that stage yet.

I remember being at a grocery store and they were doing a demonstration of some new vendor product. The demonstrator was being rather pushy and insistent that I purchase his wares. I explained to him that I needed to ask my husband what he thought, and suddenly he backed off! Either by some preconditioned chauvinistic beliefs that governed his selling strategy or by sheer luck, he decided I was not going to make a purchase, and then I walked away. This was not the only time I did this. I would have solicitors come to the door and deny them access (and a sale) because I explained that my husband made those decisions. Here I was, a modern young woman who was strong(ish) and independent, playing the dingy housewife card! It infuriated me how effective this strategy was; it infuriated me that I was continuing to use it. I often used pronouns like *we* and *us* when having casual conversations with people. Friends and family would never correct me when I did this—part of their denial of the situation, I suppose. But I found it far easier to deny the accident than to explain to people who I am.

When you tell a stranger that you are a widow, a whole spectrum of outcomes can occur. The most common, in my experience, is when the person goes wide eyed and socially awkward around you for the rest of your interaction. They stumble over their words and keep avoiding eye contact with you, you know, lest they wake your inner widow (like the Incredible Hulk or something). This reaction typically comes from folks who have never experienced a loss to this level and simply don't know how to act in this situation.

Another type of reaction I have experienced when "coming out" is one of morbid curiosity. In a feeble attempt to display empathy and understanding, the stranger now wants to become your new best friend by interrogating you about every minute detail of your widowhood. "How long ago? When did it happen? How did it happen?"

On days when it is hard enough to wake up and leave your house, these people can just ruin your day. Frankly, all of those questions are inappropriate and nobody's damn business, but if the person doesn't know any better, you have to try to let it slide. In fact, most of the interactions you will have with people after becoming a widow are rooted in well-intended ignorance. I try to remind myself that these interactions are also an opportunity to educate someone on how to handle themselves in talking with people who are grieving.

Then, once in a while, you will share your widow status with a fellow widow/ widower. When this happens, it is like two great celestial bodies meeting on the universal plane. There is steely silence, a quiet serenity that contains within it understanding and love. Your eyes meet, and it is not out of judgment or panic, but to connect. Companionship and connection are precious commodities to humanity and often go underappreciated until you are denied those things. Widows know this; widows live this. And so for the briefest of moments, you find connection again with another person. Such a profound connection can result in tears, hugs, laughter— really any emotion that surfaces that day. But with the emotion du jour is also a great comfort that you are not alone after all. For all of these reasons, I thoroughly enjoy meeting fellow widows. In fact, it was my desire to meet fellow members of the suckiest club ever that fueled me to get past the public denial of my husband's death. It took about twelve months, but eventually I was able to be honest with the world and show them who I really was: a badass widow.

## The Weeks That Followed

By the time I had confirmed Samuel's accident and death, Christmas was just six days away. There was a cruel irony in this— Christmas was not one of my favorite holidays, but now I was on a hell-bent mission to have the best damn Christmas ever! My kids got a raw deal losing their dad, especially so close to Christmas. I felt like I owed them a reason to smile and be happy. My aunt told me, "Oh, they are so little. They will be fine. They probably won't even remember this in a year or two."

I begrudgingly nodded to appease her while trying to stifle the urge to cuss her out. Looking back, I think this was her form of denial in the grieving process—that the kids would not be adversely affected by the loss.

I tried clearing my head by driving around town, which ended miserably. One panic attack sliding on some ice and two pull-over-to-cry breaks later, I finally got to the toy store. Half of our gifts were in Samuel's trunk, hiding from the kids. Now, it seemed, we hid them so well that they will never come back—just like Samuel. I laughed out loud at this thought and then felt guilty for even thinking it.

My mom was shopping with me, the whole time being patient and quiet, letting have my freak-outs and embracing me. When we picked up the replacement toys and got to the register, she could see how hard it was for me to be out, and so she asked me to wait in the car.

She came out with the bags of gifts in tears and loaded them in the trunk. Apparently, our family photo, which was used in the local news story to cover the accident, was well circulated because I was recognized by the staff when we began shopping. As I went to the car, the employees confirmed my identity with my mother and then proceeded to give us our entire purchase free of charge! My mom was worried for me and my children being in a new town with no family nearby (she had flown in for the holidays). This one act of kindness almost brought her to her knees, and myself as well.

But as we were about to drive away, feeling grateful on a level I had never anticipated, another shopper in the store stopped us to give us two additional presents they had bought for my kids. When we arrived back at my apartment, the leasing office had left us a gift card and a box full of groceries.

My head was reeling; I was still numb from all that had happened this past week. I didn't want to shout out to the world what we were going through. I had never been one to air my laundry in public. But it seemed the world already knew my business anyways, and it was helping out my kids and me. At this point, I really hated Nebraska—hated that inside of moving there four weeks prior, it had torn my family apart. But after the community supported us through the holiday season, the Midwest would forever remain in my heart.

―――――――――――――

This memory taught me two important lessons about denial. The first is that friends and family will grieve in a different flavor than our own, but that denial is still very much a part of that mourning. As my aunt demonstrated, their denial of certain challenges that need to be faced ahead is coming from a place of love and (attempted) reassurance. I truly believe that she meant well when she told me those things. But she did not understand the utter devastation that losing a parent can cause to two young children. It has been estimated that semi-healthy and stable adults can take between seven to eight years to cope with the death of a loved one—and my children's combined age was less than this! Almost three years later, my six-year-old daughter still asks about her dad and still misses him every day. My son, who was an infant when we lost Daddy, can still recognize him in photos.

Parental bonds are eternal, and as hard as it was for me to be young widow, I admittedly was in deep denial about how hard my children were taking the loss. I said and did things that probably did not help them cope or deal with their pain, and for this, I will carry guilt with me for a long time.

Fortunately, I did do a few things right. I always let them talk about Daddy, and never shut down conversations about him around the kids. I told friends and family to openly share stories about their dad with the kids and also convey to them how much he loved them both. My sister even made them memory quilts and teddy bears, which are cherished possessions to this day. Our home has a special place of honor for family members we have lost, and Samuel is prominently centered in this display. When they are older, I have saved some of his clothes and beloved mementos for them to keep as adults.

The second lesson this memory taught me was that I was in major denial about having to walk this road alone. I think, as widows, we can sometimes translate the uniqueness of our grief into being uniquely alone and isolated from the world around us. But the truth is we are not alone. Even if we are cut off from friends and family, there is a community out there ready and willing to embrace us with open arms. Many of my fellow widows have found this community in widow support groups, church/ spiritual congregations, or in seeking out new life experiences.

I am very grateful that my family is large and extends across the globe. But to be so widespread makes it challenging for same-day support. I have found that my friends have been my saving grace and helped me weather the choppy waters of single motherhood. Mind you, most of my friends now are new.

For the same reasons that strangers feel awkward and cannot interact with you, you will also experience disconnects with friends during this time for the same reasons. I am not saying it is fair or right, but there is an adage amongst widows that "your phonebook changes" after widowhood.

I suppose my final reflection on denial is this—it can always come back. Last week, I turned away a solicitor with my favorite excuse ever—my husband makes those decisions. For me, this expression of denial came from a place of exhaustion and frustration. I had had a very hard day, the kids did not behave well in school, and another unexpected bill had surfaced. My need to make the solicitor leave surpassed my Zen-like acceptance of Samuel's death. But I wasn't mad at myself this time, and for me, this screams of healthy progress. I have come to realize that any step we take in any stage of the grieving process is valid. And now, I am coming from a more reflective place where I can dissect my motivation to deny my identity. I mean even people who are not grieving feel insecure, right? So why do we put such pressure on ourselves to be perfect even in the most trying times of our lives?

It is important to know that grieving is not a checklist—once you get through one phase, there is always a chance of cycling through it again. For that matter, everyone will cycle through the stages at different rates and in a different order. Loss is not some one-size-fits-all thing. But at least I can own my loss now, at least I can share, and most importantly, at least I can acknowledge and validate my feelings instead of denying they are there.

# CHAPTER 2

# Denial of Doctors

## Imposter Syndrome and the Crap People Say

I WALKED INTO MY FIRST-YEAR residency with sweaty hands and a racing heartbeat. For me, this was it—the epitome of academic achievement and scholarly lifestyle. I was fulfilling a lifelong dream of becoming a doctor (of something), and I was doing it in my late twenties! Not only this, but I was also the first person in my family to achieve this academic level.

My back arched a little as I walked into the classroom, noticing I was the youngest person there. I met eyes with a few of my soon-to-be colleagues, each demonstrating their own versions of peacock puffery. I suppose this was the classic case of too many chefs in the kitchen—each of us intelligent, experienced, and successful. I glided into a chair in the front row, channeling my inner Hermione as I placed my materials on the desk just so. My ears were buzzing as the professor walked into the room.

A woman who looked not much older than myself and had a grin that went from coast to coast. Indeed, she welcomed us into her world with a cheery disposition and a sincerity that would be much appreciated in the days ahead.

As inviting as this preliminary period of my residency was, it did not offset the challenges and stress that was cultivated the remainder of the week. Almost immediately after we introduced ourselves, we were met with an onslaught of deep, reflective questions—questions (it was clear) no one was prepared to answer. Our professor, with her now Umbridge-like smirk, questioned everything we said, challenged every position we asserted. I began to have sweaty hands again though this time it was from anxiety and not from my Christmas-esque excitement.

At the end of day one, we all walked to our room corridors with our heads held low. Those of us that didn't wash out on the first night (of which there were three) returned to class the next morning with furrowed brows and tense movements. Our positively perky professor sauntered into the room with her grin to end all grins and raised an eyebrow as if to congratulate herself and say internally, "And then there were twelve."

We were asked to split up into small groups of three for a project that would be due at the end of the week. I was the last one to be picked for a group. I like to think it was because I was the only one who dared to sit in the front row again, but realistically, it was probably because of my age and bubbly demeanor. I have long fought people's assumptions about my competency, especially in professional circles. I am five-foot-nothing, have a chirpy voice, and smile perhaps too much for the business world. But I always hit my goals, reduce my budgets, and get things done early. I was just perhaps hoping that in academia, this perception would be different. No such luck.

As we gathered into our groups, I found myself placed with a brilliant man who had spent more years than I was alive in the criminal justice system and a woman who was pursuing this degree as a bucket list item and who did not wish to pursue academic life after graduation. For myself, I was planning on using this degree to fulfill my ultimate goal of teaching at the university level. I had worn many hats in my career, and in each one I realized that the teaching, coaching, and training aspects were my favorite elements of the job.

As I began to doubt my ability to hold my own with my partners, we were tasked with presenting a rough draft of our project within twenty-four hours. My insecurities about my expertise on the project wormed deeply into my psyche. I did not speak out on design choices I disagreed with. I did not assume a leadership role in the project. I did not even object to the unsubstantiated evidence we were using to support our arguments. I was coasting through the project, doing what I was told by the other two who were grateful that some young hotshot wasn't arrogantly swaggering around (their words).

We met for breakfast in the meal hall the next day and discussed how the presentation would transpire. The gentleman, who was at this point our appointed leader, would do most of the talking, and we would all field questions as appropriate. His bravado and nonchalant grace suggested (to me) that he knew what he was doing. At least, this was what I was telling myself since I had placed my grade (and my future in the doctoral program) squarely in his hands.

Of course, we were asked to present first. Once the initial nervous minutes had passed, I was feeling pretty confident in our presentation overall. Unfortunately, our professor felt otherwise. She ripped our supporting arguments to shreds and challenged our answers to any questions fielded from the class. We were not alone; every group faced the same fate that day in class. She recommended that we dig deeper and thoroughly read the literature we were using to support our report. She also recommended that our spokesperson change their approach—they cannot speak to things they knew nothing or very little about except to acknowledge that they didn't know anything about it.

Back in the lobby area of our rooms, we all sat around and had a big heart-to-heart about our performance that day. The personal insecurities, personal denials, personal-isms came rolling out of our mouths as if to wash away the past few days and allow us to truly meet the real us for the first time. Our lead stated that he has always had a problem with overconfidence and "fakin' it 'til you make it." My other partner acknowledged that she doesn't usually go above and beyond in a course assignment and that she had usually relied heavily on her intelligence to waltz through coursework with ease. I recognized that I had been fooling myself to not want to play a more active role in the project. We shared our personal and professional backgrounds with each other and the many motivations that led us to this point in our lives.

After this discussion, which was two hours in length, we all had a newfound sense of calm and validation. We did not feel dejected and beaten. Rather, we were newly motivated to excel and pass this residency.

Other groups did not have the same reaction. I remember one group in particular who was also trying to address the professor's concerns in the lobby. They were arguing, blaming, denying, and ignoring everything we had been taught earlier that day. Instead of being receptive to feedback, they denied its validity and remained steadfast in their self-righteous indignation. They were not actively listening to each other, let alone the professor. As their conversation drew on, the more flustered they all seemed. And the crap they were saying about the quality of each other's work was not team friendly to say the least.

It was no surprise to me when we walked into the class the next day to find that this entire group had decided not to pursue to program further. In four days, we had been reduced to nine out of fifteen students. I sympathized for the people who opted to discontinue the program. They had put in time and money and sacrifice to get here, and was it all for nothing?

When the professor walked into class, we all stiffened with anticipation of the newfound trials to occur today. But instead, our professor smiled, and this time it was similar to her gentle grin of the first day and stated, "Congratulations. You have successfully partaken in true academic discourse. We scholars question everything because we must. We support what we say with justification from other scholars, but we do so to create new knowledge for the world. And when we have a difference of opinion with one another, we are civil and open-minded to discuss and consider alternate possibilities. It is okay to say 'I don't know' just as much as it is okay to say 'It depends.' It is not easy, and it will require you to even challenge and question your own core beliefs. You will get criticism and feedback from everywhere and in every direction. Keep your integrity, do self-reflection often, and do not question whether you deserve to be here."

The last sentence resonated with me deeply. I had been in major denial about whether there was even a place for me in the upper crust of the academic world. I was raised modestly in a large family with varying degrees of professional and academic success. But I was the first in my family to even attempt pursing a terminal degree—we had no lawyers, no doctors, not even a dentist. They all thought I was crazy to try and go back to school with two small children at home. I didn't realize until the moment my professor said that I deserved to be there that all of the crap my friends, family, and coworkers were saying/ doing was actually fueling my insecurity and doubt. My denial was indeed being nourished by forces outside of my head even though it was inside of my head where all of this was being expressed.

Our professor went about the lesson the rest of the day not more relaxed and inviting again. The rest of the week was where true growth occurred for those of us that persevered. All nine of us kept in touch for years after this residency even though we were scattered around the world. We had survived the first of three crucibles together, and that bond was a pillar of support during the program. Our professor also never graded out first presentation and was very positive in the feedback and grading of our final projects at the end of the week.

As it turns out, this class was most about the soft skills needed to be a scholar rather than the topics addressed in the classroom. It was the first time in a school environment where I felt challenged, uncomfortable, and stressed. I actually had to work to pass the class because it wasn't really about a class—it was a lesson in causing a mind shift and embracing the identity of scholar.

---

Looking back, I realize that my professor was trying to let the flakes wash out before going into the core work of the residency. Doctoral students, both in online and traditional programs, have a high attrition rate. The caliber of work, critical thinking, and synthesis of information that must occur is daunting. When I graduated, they told me that I am now part of a club that less than 2 percent of the American population is included in. This blew my mind. I felt honored, humbled, and unworthy. Many people on this journey feel the same way. It is a phenomenon known as imposter syndrome (IS), and it is rooted squarely in the denial we place in our own value, worth, competency, and capability.

For those who experience IS before starting a PhD program, it can negatively influence your view of your abilities to the extent that you may prevent yourself from even enrolling in a degree program. Individuals who experience IS after graduation usually feel it when advancing professionally. Perhaps they do not feel competent enough to justify the increase in pay and responsibilities. Perhaps they question how much they have retained from their degree. For the former, the only advice I have to give is that you never know what you are truly capable of until you push yourself. For the latter, if you have completed your doctoral degree, you are part of 2 percent of the American population who can officially put "subject matter expert" in your list of skills. You have sacrificed, researched, tested, and discovered, all to get to this point in your career. All employees that are new in role will have OJT, and all new tasks will be on learning curve—do not let that psych you out of fulfilling your potential.

The story I shared was about the denial or IS I experienced during the program. I had enough self-confidence to enroll and get to my first residency. But when I was there, it immediately washed over me like a wave of negativity. It reminded me of those 1980s movies where the main character has had to overcome adversity and they are seeing/ hearing all of the insults others had given them throughout the movie. Ultimately, I realized that my professor was Mr. Miyagi, and my self-doubt was the Cobra Kai. Indeed, I deeply respect and revere my professor.

After residency, we remained in contact, and now I find myself in the rewarding position of calling her mentor and friend. As it turns out, she had finished her degree young and had children not much older than my own. We exchanged hand-me-down clothes for the kids, and she would review my papers (never pulling her punches). But it is a relationship that helped me stay the course even after Samuel's passing. She taught me at residency about two years before his accident, and she saw the changes in my life that occurred after the car accident. She respected me for taking a sabbatical from my studies to let my family reset. She was patient with me getting wishy-washy about my study (which really is a kind of fear we all face when pulling the trigger and completing each phase of our programs). But she never gave up on me, and always nudged me to keep moving forward. I may have dedicated my dissertation to my late husband, but I thanked and praised her in my acknowledgments.

Oftentimes we think we are the only one feeling a certain way. Perhaps we feel we are the only ones who finished their degree on luck and that we don't really have the qualifications to do a certain job. Or perhaps we question how strong we are to survive the death of a spouse and keep on living. In either case, we are tasked with baring our souls to the world and trusting that we are loved enough and valued enough to be accepted by society. For me, acceptance and denial go hand in hand. I couldn't get over my denial of Samuel's death until I accepted his death and what it meant to me and my life. I couldn't get past my denial about my academic status until I was accepted by other scholars in the field. Until we attain personal, internalized acceptance, we must surround ourselves by those who are accepting. In my case, I began to network with peers and faculty at my university. I kept putting my name out there. I had professors tell me my notions about my field of research were crazy; I have also had some say I am brilliant. As a widow, I joined support groups and began socializing with fellow widows. I changed many of my friends who did not appreciate or (accept) my new social status. I didn't do this to be mean. I did this to grow and heal. I just kept chiseling away at the denial in my life.

One final thought about denial: denial is uncomfortable. It is unpleasant, and it hurts us (albeit indirectly). It reminds me of an adage I heard once about lobsters. Lobsters, being crustaceans, must shed their hard exoskeletal structure as they grow. It gets very tight and cramped and uncomfortable before they finally are able to burst out of their self-made prisons and become more than they were, with more room to grow further. So in nature, discomfort can be a good thing. It can symbolize the beginning of changes that make us even more than we are now. For widows, doctors, and Dr. Widows, I say to you we should all be more like lobsters.

# CHAPTER 3

# Anger of Widows

Pain is pain is pain
It's not a competition;
It is brotherhood

No one can judge me
Gummy Bear in hair—don't care
I'm a damn widow!

Today I went pee
And the toilet seat was down
Some changes are nice

## No Marriage Is Perfect

I WAS A VERY ANGRY kid. My parents divorced when I was five. Admittedly, they were not made for each other. They got along far better as two separate entities than one unified unit. That is not to say I didn't love my parents. Nor did I ever feel unloved by them. In fact, I cannot think of two people who could have more positively shaped me into the person I am today. But as a kid, I was just pissed that almost overnight I took on the role of man of the house, helping to raise my two younger sisters. I learned to cook, clean, repair computers, kill bugs, and any other task that life had thrown at me. My mother, a nurturing woman, was single and looking for a friend and confidant. As I got older, she would oscillate the terms of our relationship back and forth between friends and mother-daughter. When friend-me made a comment she didn't appreciate, she would immediately switch back to mom mode, and I would be punished for being disrespectful or sassy. After her second marriage ended, she resolved to remain single the rest of her life, having been hurt by too many men that she had loved. And with each ended relationship or heartbreak, friend-me would fly in to give her some advice only to have it squashed by my friend-mom.

My father was absent much of my childhood, serving in the military. We would get messages and gifts from him, but face-to-face time was limited to a few times a year. This was reduced even further after his marriage to our stepmother. She was a woman who did not respect us (my sisters and I) much, having created double standards in the house for how her kids were treated versus how we were treated. My dad eventually left this woman, but not before they had a baby together, my youngest sister. I desperately wanted a relationship with her, but we were far apart both in age and geographic distance. Any attempts I had at bridging a relationship were often extinguished by her mother. On top of all of this, I had been overweight my entire childhood and had endured the typical insults, bullying, and judgment by friends, family, and doctors. I did not let it get to me; in fact, I have always had a strong sense of self and self-love. I have often found myself fat and happy versus being skinny and bitchy. But needless to say, I was pretty displeased with certain elements of my life, and I didn't really fancy myself a believer in love everlasting.

That is when I met Samuel. We were sophomores in high school and had homeroom together. I was immediately smitten with him. I am not really sure why, but he was gentle yet strong, smart yet naïve. He was also extremely clueless about girls. I gave him my phone number, and he waited until the next school year to call me. He claimed it was because he didn't know I was interested in him to which I explained that providing one with a phone number is the very definition of being interested. That was how much of our relationship was for the first ten years. Rather than admit he was clueless (or wrong), he would just ignore issues until they undoubtedly turned into bigger issues that I was asked to fix.

At first, I didn't mind—I liked teaching, and teaching the love of my life something new was sort of exciting. But as the years passed, the persistent reminders, the constant explanations, and the prescheduled Samuel meltdowns we starting to wear on me. It wasn't one or two things I was teaching him, but *everything* about being an adult. I taught him how to wash dishes, do laundry, and cook meals. I showed him how to organize a filing cabinet and draft a résumé. When his flaky friends were not doing a good job at our wedding photography, I had to walk him through how to fire people. I was angry. I was angry that the adulting of our lives was strapped to my shoulders, and I felt like I was the only one carrying the burden and feeling the strain.

Samuel grew up in a very loving home. One year, his parents dressed up as June and Ward Cleaver, and it actually fit them to a tee. His mother, by all rights a beautiful and intelligent career woman, left the professional world to have and raise Samuel. For her own reasons, she had put ungodly amounts of pressure on herself to be the best mom ever. Samuel had his three square meals a day, plus brownies, plus whatever his heart desired. His father was just as doting. I have never met two people who had more love to give. And that made me angry.

*Why?* I thought to myself. *Why did the world give me nothing but hurdles to jump when it paved a smooth road for Samuel to walk?* And it hit me like a ton of bricks—I was not angry at Samuel; I was jealous. I was jealous that he had a stable, loving home. I was jealous that his parents celebrated his existence every day. They even celebrated half-birthdays, which is the six-month mark from his previous birthday! Whereas I was barely given a pat on the back for straight As because it was simply expected that I perform well. Meanwhile, my younger sister, who was less academically inclined, was given $20 once for earning a C in a class. Long story short, Samuel and I had different lives, and that difference was starting to put a wedge in our relationship.

But having realized my anger was in fact jealousy didn't help. In fact, all it did was redirect the anger from being outward to being inward. *Why am I being a selfish, petty person? Why the hell am I jealous of past events I cannot change and have no control over?*

It took me most of my early twenties to come to terms with my own inner rage and issues. And did Samuel waiver during that time? No. Did he get angry too? Sure, but we made a promise to each other to talk out the anger and never go to bed angry. My mother assured me that this was what maturing looked like, and she said she was happy to see that we were growing together instead of growing apart.

As we began to strengthen the adult bond of our relationship and improve our communication with one another, I discovered that Samuel had a *ton* of self-doubt, which angered him. So one day, we decided to stop being angry at ourselves and start to love ourselves instead. It is amazing how powerful self-love actually is.

Loving ourselves and being happy in our own skin actually made us better equipped to love each other. But it is also amazing to see how easily anger can creep back into your mind if you let it.

Our wedding happened when we were twenty-five, and we had been together for ten years. Shortly after, we were trying to start a family. The first year we were married, I got pregnant! I was so excited for the news. But by the time we had scheduled our first doctor appointment, I had miscarried. We didn't tell anybody about it, not even our parents. I was too embarrassed and sad (and angry), and Samuel I think was simply trying to respect his wife's wishes to keep it quiet.

The next year, we miscarried again, and again the third year we were married. In our fourth year of marriage, I was the farthest along I had even been pregnant—about sixteen weeks. I remember working in the stockroom at the store I was managing at the time and feeling a sharp pain in my gut, followed by a hot gush of blood down my leg. I rushed to the bathroom to find my baby malformed and expelled from my body. I had to silently cry in the public restroom while I cleaned myself up. I walked to my office, a mere ten feet away (but felt like a mile) to call the hospital and the backup manager to explain why I was leaving the building.

When I got home that night, I finally came clean to my family. Samuel and I explained to them the four miscarriages we had excluded them from. My best friend dropped everything just to hold me on my couch while I sobbed ceaselessly. My mother came over and said nothing. She didn't need to say anything—she simply held me and rocked me the way she used to when I was little. The next day, I told Samuel that I could not handle the hurt of losing another baby. He felt the same, and we decided to pursue adoption thereafter. I hated myself for not being able to give him a child. And I hated that my sisters—who by all rights were less responsible, less financially stable, and less, well, me—were popping out babies like raindrops. My anger was back full force.

Fast-forward to 2016, and a lot had changed. We finally were able to adopt two of our foster children and were now a forever family of four! I was rocking the mom bit, and Samuel was the best dad to our children. He had grown up—*a lot*—and had landed a dean's scholarship to go to law school in Nebraska. He was even excited about moving away from his hometown for the first time ever. My anger had dissipated and was replaced with buzzing excitement for the future.

Inside of a few years, we were going to be a lawyer and a doctor, and our kids would be set for life. It was everything we had dreamed of (minus the impending doom of some student loan bills that would be due). Two days before his accident, we were cruising along on a family outing singing Christmas songs in the car. I remember thinking that things could not get much more perfect than this. Then the accident happened.

———————

After the denial phase, I immediately became enraged at his passing. At first, I hated myself as it had become one of my major personality quirks over the years. I loathed that I could have been so petty, so hurtful, and so wasteful with the precious and finite time we had together. Then I got mad at God for even inventing black ice in the first place. I got mad at the universe for allowing Samuel and I to find each other only to be ripped away from one another. And then I got mad at Samuel. I was so upset that he never learned to drive in snow (even though he was born and raised in Arizona). I was mad that he died first—we actually used to joke about who we thought would go first. He always thought it would be him, just when he was eighty or ninety. I was mad that he had left me alone to raise our children. I was upset that I was without my best friend and no longer had a companion in life. I was infuriated that he died in an accident four weeks after a cross-country move, leaving me very much alone on an island socially. I would get mad at finding his belongings, evidence of a life that once occupied this home with me. Then I would get mad at myself all over again—I actually got mad at feeling mad! So much so I thought I was going mad. In therapy, I wrote a haiku about how nice it is not to worry about the toilet seat anymore, and then I got pissed at myself for thinking that thought and became incredibly guilt riddled. Oh, I was mad at so many things.

I did not always cope with the anger well. Sometimes, I would snap at my children for no reason. After all, it wasn't their fault that a hurricane was going on inside of my head; they had no idea. I made some emotional and irrational decisions the first six months of my widowhood. I didn't drink or smoke or seek out relief with drugs (prescription or otherwise). But I did eat my feelings (again, another lifelong coping skill).

It was about April 2017 when I had finally closed out all of the affairs of my husband's estate. Every form had been signed; every account had been resolved. It was like a foggy haze that had been lingering over my head had finally been blown away with the spring breeze. I realized that my anger was many things, but most of all, it was unproductive. My kids and I couldn't carry on in this toxic negative funk the rest of our lives. It was not what Samuel wanted, nor was it what I wanted.

I decided to make some lifestyle changes. Every time I got mad, I would go for a walk or go to the gym. I fell in love with Zumba classes, and the kids were enjoying some social interaction at the gym daycare with other kids their age. I started Jenny Craig because I figured if I was going to eat my feelings, at least I could do it a low-calorie way. By 2018, I had lost a hundred pounds. Open admission here, by the time Samuel had died, I was over three hundred pounds, so this was big deal for me. And I did not lose the weight to feel prettier. (If you recall, I have always felt fabulous.) But I wanted to play and keep up with my kids. They were already dealt some pretty tough hands, and it would completely stink to become orphaned because Mommy like chimichangas too much.

I also channeled my anger back into my studies. I became driven to complete my degree since my husband could not. I wanted to show my kids that even in the face of adversity, you can do anything you set your mind to. I was able to do this because I had also moved in with my dad. He immediately became my knight in shining armor and has helped to raise my kids ever since. Without his support, none of the positive things in my life since Samuel's death would have happened. For that matter, my mother continues to show me that I can have a full, rich life as a strong single woman (which has removed a lot of thoughts about dying alone from my brain). Twenty-twenty hindsight of course, but I think all of the hurdles I have leapt in my life have helped me get to where I am now. And appreciating what I have been given, in retrospect, has helped me immensely with eliminating the anger in my heart.

So the advice I can give to my fellow widows consists of three key ingredients:

1.  **Find a safe and healthy way to express anger** – Bottling up any kind of emotion is unhealthy, and anger certainly can fester when internalized. Find a way that anger can be used to result in a positive outcome. For me, I do Zumba and play the *taiko* drums. These massive Japanese wine-barrel drums can take a beating, and they are the perfect prescription for an angry widow.
2.  **Be productive** – Idleness, in my experience, has induced periods of anger, depression, and sadness in my life. I try to keep busy (perhaps too much) with projects for my career and my kids to avoid this pitfall. But perhaps keep home or craft projects handy that you can work on as needed.
3.  **Be thankful and reflect on your blessings** – Perspective is key here. When I reflect on past events, I can hold on to

the anger I felt at the time, *or* I can appreciate the lessons it taught me in life or the opportunities it prepared me for. For example, I used to be so frustrated that I had to teach my late husband everything when we lived on our own. But now, I like to think that it was his way of letting me practice teaching our kids when the time comes for them to be independent adults. The four miscarriages I experienced were like a wound that cut deeper each time, making me feel like an inferior female. But now I have come to appreciate that losing my babies made me crave motherhood deeply. I needed that drive to remain patient and loving toward my babies while we were fostering them, waiting to see if they would be eligible to adopt.

I do not want to spout platitudes like "things always happen for a reason" because to a widow, this is a shitty thing to say (especially at the funeral for those of you reading who are not widows, but widow-adjacent). Instead, let me leave you thinking that as long as you can learn something from a life experience (positive or negative), then do not regret that it happened to you. You are who you are because of the culmination of every step you have walked. And you are beautiful, amazing, unique, and strong.

# CHAPTER 4

# Anger of Doctors

## Leaving in the Eleventh Hour

I WAS IN THE TAIL end of my doctoral program. All of my coursework had been completed. My study had been conducted; I had analyzed my data, and I was writing my final chapters 4 and 5. The last hurdle I needed to jump before my oral defense was a final quality approval, also known as QRF. When I submitted my draft to my committee, which consisted of one chair and two committee members, my chair and one committee member praised me for a job well done. They really found my findings fascinating and on the pulse for my field of expertise. They were looking forward to seeing the oral defense (which is the final test before getting to be called doctor).

The final committee member, however, felt differently and felt that somehow I had personally betrayed them by going against the original study design that was approved three years prior. In that time, the school had rearranged, realigned, reconfigured, and adjusted their entire program up to and including what my study would look like in order to graduate. So by simply accommodating current university policy, I somehow now was going against the particular opinion of *one* committee member. They had privately sent an email to my chair after I submitted my draft to them for review. My chair was livid—the contents of that email was disclosed to me including the fact that they were (1)going to disapprove my dissertation or (2) they're just going to drop out of my committee entirely, whichever my chair preferred.

Either outcome would have prevented me from graduating and put me in administrative limbo with the university. Passing the buck on my chair was not professionally courteous at all, nor was it acceptable to give up on a student that you had promised to mentor and build a relationship with for the last three years.

But they left my committee nonetheless. This committee member, by all rights, is a professional in their field and quite knowledgeable about certain methodologies, and for that, I give them credit. But where I don't give them credit is that there is a difference between being a researcher and a scholar, a teacher and a mentor. And in the latter, they failed miserably. So here I was in the eleventh hour unable to move forward until I obtained a unanimous approval from a full committee. I was dismayed. And I was disheartened. And I simply didn't know what to do.

I called my chair who had been an amazing friend and confidant over the past few years; she had been flexible and adaptable to the changes of the university as well as the changes that I needed to do to meet my work-life balance and still get my study off the ground. She suggested we get on a conference call with the other committee member, and I proceeded to do so. They did not provide me any clear help or guidance except to support what I've currently been doing and acknowledge and validate the work I've done. But even that vindication was helpful, and it was enough to give me clarity of mind to figure out that I needed to reach out to the university for help.

At this point, in my program, I had been a widow for about two years. And about twelve months into those two years, I finally figured out that sometimes I do need help, and it is okay to ask for help. So I took that lesson from my widowhood, and I applied it to my school life. I reached out to the student advocacy member of the university who was very prompt to say that they apologize for the confusion and the disheartening behavior of that particular faculty member (who would be followed up with accordingly). I had never prior had a complaint about the university, having gone there for not one but two degrees. They acknowledged that as well, realizing that this was not some whining or casual complaining or blaming game that I was trying to play. This was a legitimate issue that needed to be addressed with their help.

Within twenty-four hours, I got an email from the dean of my department with a list of faculty members that I could potentially reach out to for additional committee assistance. Thankfully, though, I'd also had a little black book created through my networking over the years since my first residency. A member of faculty that I appreciated during my coursework, one of my old professors, decided to step up for me in the eleventh hour because she knew me and she knew the quality of my work. She also knew that it would be an easy yes to help me push through the final stages of my program.

Within seventy-two hours of one faculty member showing their true colors and leaving (when essentially things got tough), I had found a replacement committee member. I was able to get my draft approved, and within a month of that, I proceeded to do my oral defense and pass. Bear in mind that up to this point in the program (and if you recall from my first residency story), I had been riddled with harsh critique and criticism and challenges and questions of my intentions. For years, I had been putting up with this type of hypercritical feedback. And yes, you do have to remain receptive to it until you learn and grow. But I'd be lying if I told you it didn't wear on me, and it was a blow to my ego at times. In fact, it was very frustrating to know that being the single parent now in my family, I was sacrificing time with my two young babies. I would hold up in my office on the weekends and type up papers only to have them rip to shreds by somebody who I'd never met in person because I was attending university online. There's a lot of anger that builds up as a result of that.

---

Being receptive to feedback was, has been, and will be one of the most maddening things about higher learning. I have worked in business for close to two decades, and I have worked entry-level roles and leadership positions. I have received my share of feedback from all sorts of professionals regarding my abilities, knowledge, and performance. Historically, I have always been praised for my ability to accept and incorporate feedback. But academia, my friends, is a wholly different animal, and she is a carnivore. First, let's call out the obvious circumstances that make critical feedback during a doctorate the most difficult news to hear.

1.  Most higher academics are fifty shades of nutty professor, resulting in a myriad of scatter-brained, overworked, underappreciated, flip-flopping feedback. As well-intentioned as their thoughts are, they are either too forgetful to keep their story straight or too exhausted to convey their notes in a compassionate manner. Students are left confused, bewildered, and frustrated with the Yoda-like cryptics of their would-be mentors.

2.  We, the students, are emotionally invested in this degree. Unlike undergraduate and even masters programs, doctorates are pursued because of highly internalized and personal reasons. I have seen graduates take pictures of their dissertation as if it were a newborn baby. They attempt

to immortalize its words, similar to how we would bronze a baby's booties. And like actual proud parents, any criticism or harsh word about our baby is met with tension, disregard, and a defensive attitude. This preconditions most students to not be open and receptive to feedback.

To the first issue, I say that we need to understand that our faculty members are humans. Before we jump off the deep end of the despair pool, perhaps it is worth taking the time to send a clarifying email. If you are receiving poor feedback and no communication, then at least you can forward all of your unanswered messages to the student advocacy representative at your university. There is also no rule that says you cannot shop around for a second opinion from other faculty. Certain universities may restrict who gives you final approval of your work, but in the meantime at least, you can feel validated by a working scholar and stave off the risk of insanity.

For the second issue, I defer back to learning how to be receptive to feedback. Believe it or not, the shredding of your work is not actually about you, so don't take it personally. A professor may be attacking your argument, your research, or your study design choices, but those things are not you. Your dissertation, for that matter, is not you. It is not your pinnacle or your magnum opus. All too often, students walk into a program envisioning a dissertation that is consummate of their life's work, but in reality, a dissertation is a paper that represents our ability to think about problems, research problems, study those problems, and create new information that may help address those problems. Nowhere in a dissertation does it have to mention "and based on these findings, feel free to judge my merit and value as a person."

Sure, some folks may think that way, but perhaps these are the types of academics whose opinion you should take with a large grain of salt. If we cannot learn to not take things personally, then the anger will fester and build up over time.

There's a lot of anger that builds up while pursuing a doctorate. But there's also just a lot of anger amongst the doctoral community that I don't understand. Again, it's a classic case of too many chefs in the kitchen. Everyone has their own opinions and their own egos to bolster—sort of like my epic fail of a committee member. And some people prefer to do that by knocking down the work of others, which is simply inappropriate and unfair at this caliber of critical thinking. But nonetheless you'll see online support groups, for example, of doctoral students and doctoral graduates who get into pissing matches about whose university is better or more rigorous and why, which program is more valid and why, and so on. Frankly, I think anyone who is crazy enough to enter into a terminal degree program of any kind, online/ traditional/ professional degree/ philosophical degree, anything, and has the gumption to finish it and see it through deserves respect in my eyes. Everyone has an opinion about everything, and it creates a lot of unnecessary anger.

I have to go back to lessons I learned in widowhood about trying to look at other perspectives. Trying to forgive and feel sorry for people is a far more divine emotion to have than anger and jealousy and feeling betrayed. The faculty member that left my committee, I do not harbor negative feelings toward. I do not know what life situations they were experiencing at the time that might have influenced or led them to drop out. I feel sorry for them because since graduating twelve months ago, I've been published in domestic and international scientific journals. I have presented in the United States and overseas on my research and my work. I've started my own website, my own editing and consulting company for doctoral students who need extra TLC, and I will be published in three separate book anthologies in the next twelve months. Not to mention the very book you're reading is something that I decided to publish on my own.

This type of productivity would not have happened if I wasn't the person I was, and my work speaks for itself. So again, I just feel sorry for that faculty member because at this point in my life, I realize that I am an excellent asset to have in terms of a friend and colleague, and they're missing out on that. I forgive them for doing what they did. But it didn't keep me down. I kept moving forward.

## CHAPTER 5

# Bargaining of Widows

You are no longer;
Who do I have to assault
To bring you back home?

You are not deceased.
You are just out getting forms
To divorce my ass.

Please take me instead!
Won't you please take me instead?
God, take me instead . . .

## The Lesser of Two Evils

THE FIRST NIGHT SAMUEL WENT missing was really hard. I lay in bed sobbing while my dad watched my children. When my kids were in bed, I kept saying to myself out loud, almost in a hyperventilating panic, "Let him divorce me. Let him leave me. Let him say terrible cruel mean things to me. Let him say the Midwest is not for him, and he just wants to move home. He doesn't want to be a lawyer. He doesn't want to do anything with his life related to how we've planned it together. Let him do all those things. Just let him come home. Let him be alive."

That was really the first bargaining-type reaction I had, to let him divorce me but keep him alive. The second bargaining reaction I had with Samuel was to take me instead. There are far too many memories that I can recount in this book, but Samuel was by far the better human being than I was. He was well liked, well respected, and all of his accolades were well deserved. He was patient, kind, and had a gentle voice. And I was the yin to his yang. I was brash, judgmental, a hothead, very quick to argue. I came from a very feisty and loud family, and that's how I communicated with the world. To be frank, what he saw in me I still don't know. But I remember many times saying that it should have been me instead of him. I would trade my life for his in a heartbeat.

As I lay in bed quietly mumbling to myself, I found some solace and sheer exhaustion and fell asleep. The emotional toll that I had endured in those last four hours was harder than I had thought because my body immediately went into a deep dream state. And it was in this deep dream state that I met my husband again. There were no words that were exchanged between the two of us. He literally was floating above me in the bed. He gave me a hug and then did something that was very unique and special to him. He caressed my right breast. Not in a groping, feeling kind of way but almost as a way to shake my hand and say goodbye. And I knew it was him because, for reasons I won't go into in this book, the right one was his favorite. And so for him to pick that one in particular, my dream had some significance for me. He floated away and dissipated into the universe, becoming part of the space between things.

I woke up the next morning feeling like bargaining for his life was not going to be productive. It was not going to work. And it gave me a brief moment of clarity during the weekend that we were trying to figure out where he had gone. I made breakfast for my children. Of course, at this point, I was not eating at all. I started to think about other bargains that could be negotiated or brokered with the universe to find out Samuel's fate. Because by day two of him missing, I was less concerned about whether he lived or divorced me and just more concerned about finding out where he was and what had happened. The unknowns are devastating. So I began to bargain. I even bargained with the deputy sheriffs to see if there was some way I could get them to work late over the weekend and try to find out more information about Samuel. But everyone had their due diligence and their procedures they must follow and things just take time, and the rational side of my brain knew this and understood this, blah, blah, blah. But the other side of my brain was kicking and screaming in a padded room, in a straitjacket going mad.

Bargaining was also a very useful tool for me in the next twelve months after his passing, in particular with parenting the kids. At this point, I had a two-year-old and a three-year-old in my hands who were missing Daddy. They did not understand a lot about how to express anger. They knew happiness, sadness, and they were starting to learn how to trade toys. Essentially, they were bargaining with consumer goods. So I began to bargain with them: "Please, guys, let's get through today. Let's get through today without melting down and crying. If you guys can help Mommy, be happy and remember that today is going to be a new adventure. Then Mommy will get you a new toy at the end of today," or "Mommy will get you an ice cream" or some other things.

These little bargains, I told myself, we're not spoiling my kids. They were minor sacrifices for our overall wellness and sanity. I actually had somebody try to mom-guilt me at a grocery store when I was letting my kids eat some marshmallows while we were shopping. Right out of the bag in true classy form, and admittedly a snapshot of me from an outsider's perspective would not have told our whole story. But I leaned over to that mom and whispered in her ear that while I may be teaching my kids it's okay to snack on marshmallows in the grocery store, she's teaching her children how to be raving bitches and judge perfect strangers whose background they have no idea about. I then proceeded to let her know that my children are mourning the loss of their dad and I my husband. And since misery loved company, she'd be welcome to have a marshmallow too because it must be a pretty damn miserable woman who would judge somebody like this. After she turned sheet white and immediately sped out of the aisle that we were shopping in, I actually smiled. The kids were happy.

---

They were getting all hopped up on Samuel treats. But Mommy was strong for a brief moment in that foggy haze of becoming a widow. The sun parted the clouds. and I was me again. I was feisty and a loud mouth. It's amazing to think how many widows internalize the judgment and the guilt that people put on them like it is their fault their spouse died, and it is their fault their spouse got cancer. Realistically, death happens to us all. And with a very rare circumstance that usually makes court TV, we are not responsible for our spouses' deaths. We try to bargain the terms of our existence anyway. What I say to my fellow widows here is this bargaining is inevitable. It's one of the mechanisms that we use to cope with our lack of control or sense of control in situations where we clearly have none. Embrace the bargaining and make it positive, and do not feel guilty for doing it.

In my case, I made major motherly concessions with my children, but not forever just for a brief amount of time because it kept us on an even keel. It kept us from falling off the precipice of sanity and health and well-being and all the other things that we were teetering on at the time. A bag of marshmallows is well worth keeping my kids cool and calm and me cool and calm versus losing my cool and calm, snapping at my children in public, and making a scene at a grocery store for no reason—all these outcomes are far worse than the Samuel treat that I decided to bargain my children with that day.

But beyond that, we can bargain in other ways. Make bargains with yourself. Look in the mirror and say if you can get through today without breaking down, then you get a treat. "If you can get through today . . ." For example, in my case, I told myself if I could get through today without feeling angry at somebody who doesn't know my business, then I could get a treat. And these treats were not always food. Although, those were the instant-gratification winner. But this could be getting a pedicure or a massage, taking myself out for the weekend on something like a fishing trip, having a staycation. These are treats we can give ourselves as part of the bargaining process.

I think bargaining is our feeble attempt at taking control of the situation. Similar to how denial just doesn't acknowledge that it (death) exists, bargaining is our version of universal pretend where we can actually change our fates and control circumstances around us that simply are not within our grasp. I've met quite a few widows and support groups over the years who became widowed under different circumstances than myself. In particular are widows from acts of suicide or widows who survive being caregivers of the terminally ill or those with cancer and the like. Bargaining happens for every widow, and it looks very different for each type of us that are out there.

In the case of suicide, I've met a woman whose husband had committed suicide because he finally succumbed to the depression caused by extreme amounts of childhood trauma and abuse. And for that particular woman, she never wanted to trade her life for his. Instead she wanted his abuser's life to end—letting the abuser live was an injustice and unfairness that did not seem right to her. And that was the bargain she was willing to strike.

For people who are caregivers of the terminally ill, sometimes the bargain is not even for a life. Sometimes it's for more time. Just one more day with the one they love, or just give them one day without pain and suffering, and they'll do anything to make that happen.

The level of bargaining and sacrifice that each widow puts upon themselves and the pressure to fulfill those bargains varies from person to person. But all of them are significant, and all of them are important. It is also important to remember that we must acknowledge in a healthy way that sometimes, no matter how much bargaining we do, things cannot change. Cancer will not get cured overnight. My husband is never coming home from his car accident. That is a hard thing to accept.

I have been a widow three years now, and the bargaining continues. On my rough days with the kids, my tiring days with work, or my days where something triggers my grief, I bargain. "Hey, kids, if you stop fighting, we can get pizza" even though the reality is I am too tired to cook, and too distraught to parent.

"Come on, Zarina, write one more chapter without crying, and you could dye your hair blue." Incidentally, I have a blue hair. I come from two long lines of proud Asian and Celtic woman. For the former, I play the *taiko* and awaken my inner badass. For the latter, the Celts would paint their hair and bodies blue for strength, and women warriors amongst the Celts were the stuff of legend. So my new positive and healthy bargain to myself is to keep moving forward. "If you keep moving forward, then you can continue to rock at life and be a strong blue-haired warrior." Best. Bargain. Ever.

# CHAPTER 6

# Bargaining of Doctors

## Academic Needs and Wants

THE EVOLUTION OF MY DISSERTATION was something that would have turned Darwin's stomach. My initial vision of my dissertation and the final product became two very different things, and arguably the final paper was much more simplified in comparison to its original design. In my first year, I had wanted to conduct a mixed-methods exploration of generation Z in the workplace. I was immediately met with pushback and challenges from faculty. Among their top concerns, my favorite was the fact that mixed-methods studies are too hard and too time consuming to do. Instead, it was strongly recommended that I pick either a qualitative or a quantitative study. It was mentioned on more than one occasion that I shouldn't try to reinvent the wheel. I tried to bargain with my mentors, saying that it would be the best damn mixed-methods study they had ever seen, but my ill-fated self-promotion was ineffective. So I settled for a quantitative design. I had been doing business analytics for quite some time, and numerical analysis came very natural to me. I informed my counselor, and the quantitative research courses were assigned to my schedule.

Fast-forward a year or so, and I had completed all of my quantitative courses. My design was ready to be approved so that I could pass IRB and collect data. But there was a problem—my study was not aligned. You see, I had kept my original problem statement and my research question, but I had picked the methodology that did not properly align to such a problem. Of course, I did not realize this until after I had completed most of my coursework (in the wrong direction). So I was left with another choice, another compromise, another bargain. On the one hand, I could reword the problem statement, reword the research question, and force the study into a quantitative design. I really wanted to do this—it by far was the path of least resistance. Instead of rewriting 75 percent of my paper, I would only need to adjust 20 percent.

But this damned annoying voice in my head kept fighting me. I will name this voice Gertrude. Gertrude is that friend who walks around with perpetual walking bitch-face, telling you the things you don't want to hear (even though ultimately you know she is right). Well, ol' Gertie told me to not take the easy road, that even though it was what I wanted, doing a qualitative study was what I needed. For the record, sometimes I really hate Gertrude.

I struggled for a long time about this decision. But I got to the point in the program where I could not move forward without knowing which direction my study was going. At long last, I bit the bullet and realigned my study to be qualitative.

My forms were signed and approved, and I found myself in a dangerous position. How could I actually conduct a qualitative study without having learned how to do qualitative research? This question, which seemed to glaringly obvious to me *after* making such a huge decision, was not even in my periphery *before* (you know, when I was arguing with Gertrude). At this point, I could (1) waste a ton of time and money taking the courses I needed to learn the methodology or (2) go out of my way in my personal time to learn as I go. It was at this point that I became widowed. It was also at this point that Gertrude reared up her butter face to me and said, "What do you want, and what do you need?"

What I wanted to do was curl up and die, like my husband. But what I needed was to finish this program as quickly as possible so that I could provide for my children. That is when I made the biggest bargain of my life: learn qualitative research on the fly to graduate as quickly as possible, and then I can blow some of the life insurance money on a Disneyworld trip for myself and the kids. It was a huge motivator for me—Disneyworld was where Samuel and I honeymooned, and we had always talked about taking the kids there to celebrate one day. I could not think of a better bargain than this.

I began to purchase books on qualitative research, attend webinars from method experts, and even participate in conferences centric to qualitative study. By the time I was finished with my dissertation, I had read more about the methodology than I had read about the topic of the study. My eyes hurt, my head hurt, and my fingers were bleeding from all of the typing and head scratching. But the hard work paid off. My study was approved, and I published an article in an international journal about the innovations I had made in the qualitative design of my dissertation.

For a numbers girl, I had turned into some kind of qualitative methodologist—I couldn't believe it! I was so proud of myself, having bargained up instead of down, making choices for my family's needs while maintaining my work ethic and integrity. And as for Disneyworld, we are heading there in 2020 for an all-expense paid trip of a lifetime. I owed it to my kids and to Samuel. And I owe it to bargaining as a doctoral student.

Doctoral students are asked to sacrifice, compromise, and bargain constantly. This is not just from the university, but from friends, family, and work as well. Our time is precious, our energy finite; there is simply not enough resources at our disposal to do everything all at once. And so we must decide between quantity and quality, convenience or perseverance. In addition to having to compromise on our time and our resources and our energy and the love we have to give to the world and how much time we can research and sit on our computer and type, we also have to make bargains and choices about what we're willing to do for our study.

This is something that every professional scientist or researcher must ask themselves. At some point, it becomes an ethical issue. You don't want to round too many corners of course, and you don't want to compromise the integrity of what you're doing. But you are only human after all. And these decisions must be made for some students.

This includes encouraging participation with some form of an incentive. For others, it's hiring an editor. Each has its pros and cons. Obviously hiring other experts to do the work for you tiptoes on the edge of being unethical. You're going to school to learn how to do this for yourself. But if you don't have time in the day to go through your APA formatting for the 800th time, and you're at your wit's end, perhaps hiring an editor will be your saving grace to continue and finish the program. Everybody has different needs. But please keep in mind that for every shortcut made, for every article skimmed (versus read through), for every outsourced step of this process, *you* are still ultimately responsible for knowing your study top to down, left to right, and inside out.

Doctoral programs have changed over the years, but the oral defense, in my opinion, is a cornerstone to the process. It is the final lap of the race, your swan song to being a novice researcher, and it is in the defense that your knowledge (or lack thereof) becomes quite apparent.

Please also remember when making bargains and brokering editing contracts that not all editors are created equal. Not all statisticians will be an expert at the calculations you need for your study. As with anything else in a doctoral journey, do your research before paying ungodly amounts of cash to people who are supposed to make your life easier. For that matter, understand that editing takes time—do not pay for editing of an assignment that is due in twelve hours and expect flawless perusal of your work. It is just not going to happen. Moreover, editors may have a fundamentally different style, philosophical belief, and/or expectations of your work than your chair. In these circumstances, it would be prudent to follow the feedback of your chair (since, you know, they are the one who is controlling your fate). Again, there are pros and cons to utilizing these types of à la carte services. Please handle with care, and take feedback with a grain of salt.

I encourage people to keep a researching journal and remain reflective, open, and honest to themselves because it is in those moments when you have outstanding thoughts of clarity and you are more able to make a decision that best suits you and your situation. The twisted cynic in me says that if you are your own worst critic, then getting harsh feedback from faculty would not seem so bad, especially considering you have already ripped your own work to shreds, so the points they bring up will not be anything you haven't already thought to address. It is also nice to be able to reflect with a peer. Having a comrade-in-arms serve as a sounding board and another pair of eyes can be extremely helpful. Does this mean you will be doomed to failure if you are not keeping a journal or utilizing peer-review relationships? No, of course not. But I daresay you may find yourself experiencing more moments of heartache from feedback on your work than folks who maintain a continual learning or growth mind-set.

Critical reflection is also key to understanding how we can best motivate ourselves. Simply put, if you don't know who you are or what you desire, how can you motivate/ convince yourself to accomplish tasks? Bargaining does not work unless we understand all the variables of the equation. So conduct a self-inventory of the skills you possess that can be leveraged to meet your goals. Identify what challenges you will face and determine a few ways you can mitigate or avoid those pitfalls. And remember that bargaining, compromise, and sacrifice (though needed) will still cost you something, be it time, money, or your integrity. It is like my grandfather William used to say to me, "Kid, in the business world, fast, cheap, or correct, you only will ever get to have two out of the three as any point in time. If you want something fast and cheap, it won't be correct. If you want something fast and correct, it won't be cheap. And if you want something cheap and correct, it won't be fast."

In my experience, it was clear that I was willing to do my program as cheap and as correct as correct as possible. Of course, it did take me a year longer to complete than I had anticipated. So I chose to sacrifice time for quality. Some folks out there may have to do the opposite. Like I said, I do not know or understand the situation of anyone by myself. All I can recommend is to heed my advice, and no matter what you do, do not opt to sacrifice your standards of integrity. Politicians get a bad reputation of being manipulative, mutable, and corrupt—we don't need this image to become the norm in academia.

# CHAPTER 7

# Depression for Widows

Where did my love go?
Will I ever be able?
How can I manage?

Empty my vessel.
Hollow is my heart, weak my fight.
Hardened is my skin.

I think I feel it . . .
That flicker of life and love . . .
Nope, I feel nothing.

## Widowhood: The First Two Years

THE SHERIFF'S DEPUTIES HAD JUST told me about Samuel's accident the day before. I got up out of bed, mostly out of habit and not out of will. I began lumbering along like one of those post-apocalyptic zombies, going through the motions of life in my teeny, tiny apartment with my teeny, tiny children. They got fed. They were playing. Fortunately, they had each other to interact with because I was all but useless. Dad, who had at this point moved in with me, went out to grab some Chinese food because he said I had to eat. It had been almost three days since Samuel disappeared; three days of no appetite. Some knee-jerk widow reaction kicked in, and I said, "If you are going to get Chinese, then get me combo number 17."

This was Samuel's favorite, a curried Singapore noodle dish that made the whole apartment smell repugnant, but it was his favorite nonetheless. When he arrived back at the funny farm, I stood at my kitchen counter, forcing down each bite as my dad watched me like a hawk to make sure that I was actually taking in some type of nutrition and food.

After that, I lay back down on the couch curled up in my blanket and began to spiral downward into one of the deep dark depression states that I've ever been in in my life. I remember the first time it happened I was younger. Samuel and I had been married less than a year, and we just miscarried our first baby. It was not a place I wanted to be. I did not see the light at the end of the tunnel. There was no rainbow after the storm. It was just sitting in the eye of the motherfucking storm with chaos all around me and some quiet stillness, with me at the epicenter of this horrible situation that is now called my reality. When I miscarried the first time, I blamed myself. I didn't have the right work-life balance or healthy lifestyle choices, or maybe there was some immoral thing I had done, and this was just my karmic retribution of that. I also blamed myself for not being woman enough to carry a child. There is a running joke in my family, since I had long replaced my dad as the man of the house when they got divorced, that I was more like a dude than I was a chick. While this actually complimented our marriage perfectly, the thought that I was less than a woman or less than female struck a huge blow to my psyche every time I miscarried.

Samuel, by far, was more sensitive and somewhat effeminate by comparison, but we were a match made in weird heaven. He would cry at movies, and I would fix our plumbing, and it worked for us; we were happy. But as I heard the doctor explain that the miscarriage took place, I remember just hating myself—not hating the world, not hating the circumstances, just hating myself.

It was no different when Samuel died. The day after the accident, all I could think about was what a shitty wife I had been to him. We had been married six and a half years, dated and known each other half of our lives. And every single clip or argument or frustration, everything came flooding in all at once. The poor attempt to bargain with the powers of the universe for Samuel's life, the fact that I had two lovely children left with a mommy who didn't like hugs, it pissed me off that somebody subpar like me would come out on top. And he was no longer with us. In my heart, I truly believe Samuel was the type of man that would have made the history pages had he been around just a little bit longer.

My guilt and self-loathing continued for several weeks. To be frank, Christmas and New Year's remain a blur because mentally I was in a perpetual fog. My kids had grandpa who blessedly was holding down the fort. But it felt like I had nobody, like my soul had been cleaved in two, and that I was never going to see the other half again. By the four-month mark, I was well into a routine of guilt, anger, guilt, self-loathing, workout, rinse, repeat. I would wake up, field phone calls about Samuel's estate, process paperwork for the twelfth time to a company who had no idea how to handle widowhood, go cry in my room, and take care of my kiddos.

I had decided to take a brief leave of absence from my studies to get through the first six months of this shit show, and I was even feeling guilty and mad at myself for wasting time in my program. My mother kept trying to reassure me that I was doing great, all things considered, and that I shouldn't be too hard on myself.

My personality had changed. I was tired often, irritable, and antisocial. This was the polar opposite of my normal vivacious self, a textbook Leo with an ENTJ personality type. And of course, the more inward I withdrew, the worse the guilt and anger and sadness became. I never had suicidal thoughts. It was the one saving grace of my depression. I knew in my heart it would not honor Samuel's memory, nor would I be able to care for *our* kids if I died. So I kept trooping on one foggy day at a time.

At six months, school had restarted, and it too became an outlet for me. Or rather, delving into school was a good enough reason to remain antisocial and reclusive. My life existed now as a nurture unit for my children and to learn and study. It reminded me of the movie *Bicentennial Man* where the android walks around repeating that he was "happy to serve." Only I wasn't happy, and I don't know how much I was actually serving my family by turning into a disengaged robot.

At seven months, it was my birthday and our would-be seventh anniversary. My mom came out to visit, and I remember crying in her arms at the hotel between discussion posts for school. I knew for my own sanity that I needed to change my perspective. Feeling angry or sorry or not feeling at all was not healthy. I couldn't afford therapy, so I did what any broke struggling adult would do: I went to Facebook. I typed the word *widow* into the search field, and I was amazed at how many resources, groups, and services were available for people like me. At this point, I was still viewing people like me as survivors of some sort of disease rather than people who were in similar stages of their life to me. It made sense. After all, most people don't touch widows with a ten-foot pole, so of course I would begin to feel like I was ill or damaged in some way. But as I skimmed the list of widow support groups offered online, my heartbeat quickened. Could I actually be excited about something again? Was this the next step for me?

I joined three groups that appeared to have similar traits to me—raising kids as single parents, younger, and having dark senses of humor. The first day my membership was approved, I introduced myself and was welcomed to the "shittiest club ever" by 185 people. There was no judgment, no lies, no empty platitudes about remaining strong. It was honest, it was raw, and it was a mix of bitterness and hope. All of these people were living what I was living or had found a way to live past it.

By the eight-month mark, I was logging on every day to talk with new friends and even found myself starting to give advice to the newer members of our group. I don't know why, but by helping others, it felt as though I was helping myself. So for a while, my social circles were largely virtual—both from online support groups and from online classes.

I tried to compartmentalize my life. Most of my classmates had been friends with me since the start of our program years ago, yet none of them knew I was a widow. For that matter, none of my support group friends knew I was going to school. For me, I didn't want the emotional pity from my peers once they knew I was grieving. I simply wanted my work to speak for itself. I also did not want my widow friends to be intimidated or shy away from our friendship because of this whole doctor thing. I had heard about folks in the past losing relationships or professional bonds because of this intimidation factor. But at some point, I had reached a breaking point, and I needed advice from *all* of my friends about my life. I asked the widows if any of them was trying to complete college. I asked the soon-to-be doctors if any of them had lost a spouse. To my surprise, I began receiving support and advice from people who were more similar to me than I thought. I wasn't alone. There was a group of us—Dr. Widows.

Things were finally on an upswing. I wasn't crying myself to sleep at night. My kids were starting to remember their potty training (because when Daddy died, they experienced major developmental regressions). We were even putting a down payment on a home and getting out of the teeny, tiny apartment. But then came my first major trigger: Samuel's first death anniversary. Ugh. It hit me like a ton of bricks, being hurled downhill, by a Mack truck. All of the progress I had made was shattered, and I cried that whole weekend. I ran to the arms of my dad, who like me was not a hugger. But we awkwardly embraced regardless, and I began to feel a bit better.

He reminded me that it was the holidays, something Samuel loved, and that I owed it to my kids for them to have a great Christmas. I immediately went back into numb robot automation to provide the appropriate holiday cheer for my kids. My daughter, my three-year-old began to have nightmares around the same time. When I asked her what was wrong, she said, "I dream Daddy."

And that's when I knew she was being triggered too. I decided to woman up. My maternal instinct to help my daughter work through her triggers had motivated me to process and get over my own. We began to talk more openly about Daddy and our feelings about Daddy. Every Sunday, we would go to a French patisserie (Samuel was of French-Canadian descent), pick out his favorite treat (chocolate cake), and go sit and talk to him at the tree where the accident was. I would like to say that I started doing this as a benefit for the kids, but truthfully, we all needed and enjoyed this quality time. The kids would blow Daddy kisses in heaven, and I would see how much the tree was healing from the accident. It was weird to imagine that the tree could survive the accident that Samuel could not. But it was also nice to see the world was healing, and in some small way, we were too. We continued this tradition on for another six months until the kids told me that they didn't need to come talk to Daddy tree anymore although they assured me that it was quite all right to still keep buying chocolate cake every week.

So there I was, eighteen months strong as a widow, and I was finally feeling like I had my head screwed on straight. But then, my daughter started preschool, and it was another trigger. Samuel was missing all of it—their lives, our life, everything. It was heartbreaking, and I didn't want to keep experiencing new things without him. But I knew ultimately that life goes on, was going on, all around me. My kids were thriving and beginning to start school. It should be a time when I was excited, not depressed. So I decided to utilize a new mantra in my daily routine. It was inspired by my grandmother, another widow. She is quite old now and still retains a zest for life and a love of her family that I aspire to do. Every time I asked her how she was doing, her response was a simple matter of fact: "Well, I'm not dead yet."

This phrase always made me smile because, of course, I was thankful I wasn't dead yet, but there was an empowering energy about saying it out loud. So in honor of my grandmother's take on the universe and her well-being, I began stating to myself and to others that "I am living the dream."

Some people took this comment to be ironic or sarcastic while others (mostly those who have experienced personal tragedy themselves) smile and agree with some variation of "as it should be" as a response. I remember a few weeks after coining my new catchphrase that there was a small box unearthed in my home from high school. In it was a bucket list of things I wanted to do before I turned thirty, and a notebook of my doodles and sketches. The bucket list items included traveling the world, owning a car, owning a home, having a family, and paying off my student loans. I came to a revelation while reading the list that none of these things explicitly mentioned or needed a husband to accomplish. In fact, it was Samuel's passing that helped me become debt-free, and for that matter, I would not have had a family without him in my life. I felt as though he was sending me cosmic support to do the things I had always wanted to do, and that was a great comfort.

The first sketch in the book was a torn-off notebook cover with a graphic branding of my name: Dr. Zarina Garrison. I had wanted to marry Samuel since high school, and so it made sense to me to place his name in this picture. But I forgot that I had also wanted to be a doctor, and it made me cheerful to see my foresightedness in this picture. Even though he wasn't here anymore, I really was living the dream.

---

So let's put this question out there (that no doubt some of you readers are asking), "Why is this the longest chapter of the book?" Isn't this book about self-discovery and healing? Why linger so long on depression? Let me address these concerns with my own insight on grief and depression. Firstly, this is one area of Dr. Kubler-Ross's stages of grief model that I don't fully agree with. Indeed, you experience depression as a part of grief, but it is comparatively so much more monumental than pegging it simply as a stage. For me, depression was occurring *while* I was navigating through all the other stages. It was an ever-present shadow that loomed in my life (and to some extent, still does). Now, to her credit Dr. Kubler-Ross originally developed the five stages of grief before we knew what we know now about depression, and she has continued to evolve and adapt her research around this topic. But there were some *big* notions about depression I discovered on my own that I think we need to explore further:

1. **Depressed people can feel happiness.**
2. **Depression is not a stage; it is a new normal.**
3. **Embracing depression and getting outside support can help reduce its symptoms and side effects.**

If you look at depression as a state of being rather than an emotion that can be captured in a snapshot, then it makes sense that people who are suffering from depression have sporadic moments or pockets of happiness in their lives. This is a blessing and a curse—a blessing because we desperately need to feel those moments of joy amidst our own anxiety and pain, but it is a curse because in these fleeting moments of happiness, our loved ones can assume we are no longer hurting, no longer needing support. For me, I had tremendous guilt about being happy, especially in the first six months after Samuel passed away. Widows (or at least "good" widows) aren't supposed to be happy, right? Well, who in the hell makes these rules of widowhood? Where does it state our official code of conduct? The truth is that there is no one way and no right way to be a widow. If this is the only thing you get out of this book, remember: *you do you*. And remember that it is okay to feel again—feel happy, feel loved, feel excited—because it is an integral part of the journey we are still taking. You wouldn't cut your foot off while hiking because you hit some rocky terrain, so why do we cut ourselves off from feeling emotions in life when we experience adversity?

Depression, like widowhood, is a new normal. That handy fictitious rule book you received about adulting and the real world, well, all of those rules get tossed out the window. Nothing is the same. For me, food didn't even taste the same! My childhood favorites from my mother and grandmother no longer appeal to me. But I think if you go into depression thinking it is a stage (and it will pass), you may end up feeling disappointed when the shadow doesn't ever fully lift. It is too high an expectation to think that something as fundamentally effed up as losing a spouse will simply go away. We are the cumulative result of all of our thoughts, experiences, and beliefs. It is part of your identity now, this tragic event. Denying the depression, or denying its lasting presence, can be just as detrimental as succumbing to depression. Dealing with depression is a tightrope walk. On one side, you have total and utter denial (which can lead to issues of burnout and lack of self-care), and then on the other side you have letting depression win (resulting in other extreme outcomes like suicide or becoming the perpetrator of abuse/ neglect).

People suffering from depression must master the skills of coping, and how we all cope looks very different. Again, *you do you*, and find someone in your life who respects and appreciates you for taking this journey. Perhaps this is not a relative, maybe a close friend, or maybe a new friend from a support group. But find someone who will encourage you during your lows and help you sustain the highs when they occur. And sincerely give this person permission to call you out in moments when you are doing harm to yourself or to others. For me, my dad has always been someone that speaks directly; he on more than one occasion has reminded me that I needed to get out of bed or take care of my kids or simply to smile and have a good day. Find a support pillar that works for you.

# CHAPTER 8

# Depression of Doctors

## I Am Done, Now What?

MY DOCTORAL JOURNEY WAS A long and rocky road. Did I graduate on time? No. Did I get to conduct the study I had originally planned? No. Were all of my student loans paid off by the time it ended (which was the original plan)? No. Did I have a sweet job or promotion lined up after I graduated? No. The long and short answer for all of these questions was a big, fat *no*.

The day I was scheduled to present for my oral defense, I was crying in my car, trying to find a hotspot because we had just relocated across country (again), this time to the Pacific Northwest, and I needed to do my oral defense on Skype, like, fifteen minutes ago. My dad, my new live-in au pair and roommate, had accepted a job transfer for his work, resulting in a move that required I lug two children for three days in a moving vehicle while wrapping up the final stages of my program. The Internet and other utilities that were promised to be available upon our arrival were not; the new home I had purchased had a broken window in it the day we moved in;

and the little cherry on top of this poo sundae was the fact that my laptop had crashed on the road trip to get to the Pacific Northwest. The last seventy-two hours of my doctoral journey were comprised of me driving around town from various Starbucks and McDonald's with two toddlers in car seats in a feeble attempt at landing a strong enough stream to do my oral defense. To top this off, the originally scheduled time for my defense was cancelled because one of my committee did not factor in time zone changes.

But by the grace of God, and the friendliest next-door neighbor I have ever had, I was able to do my actual defense in the living room of a stranger's home while my children tormented her cats in the other room. And to be honest, all of the buildup and pressure I had placed on the oral defense was sort of anticlimactic. My committee and chair each asked me one question. They did not grill me as I had imagined. They did not question my every choice and decision in the study design like I had been conditioned to expect based on *every* previous interaction I had had with these people. Instead, they muted me for a few minutes to discuss my study and then congratulated me by stating, "Congratulations, Dr. Garrison."

They had already discussed the caliber of my work in the weeks prior since I had to locate and secure a final committee member (remember Mr. Eleventh Hour?), and so they knew that my study was solid and that I was able to convey eloquently my study to other members of academia. All of these reasons they were explaining to me after the magical words *Dr. Garrison*, but none of which were resonating with me in the moment. I was elated. I was numb. I was sort of . . . depressed it was all over. What!

How could that be? Why was I sad to be done with school? What the hell was wrong with me? I thought I was weird; okay, well, I knew I was weird, but I thought I was the only student in the history of doctoral learning that was sad to be done with my studies. By this point in my life, I was relying on online support groups daily for my personal and academic needs, so I put the question out there: "Why am I so sad to be done with school?"

The immediate onslaught of responses was amusing, inspiring, surprising, and unexpected. People answered with short trite comments like "student loans." Some even explained that I was experiencing some form of scholarly Stockholm syndrome, having fallen in love with my academic captors over time. But a few people detailed that they had felt depressed after their programs because this was the one thing in their lives that they were doing for themselves and once it ended, that magical (albeit demanding) endeavor was there no more. Did I feel that way? Did I miss the typing at 3:00 a.m. while my babies slept? Did I yearn to be torn down with red ink and corrections on a discussion post? Did I miss the dazed and confused looks of passersby when I tried explaining what I was studying?

I decided to review my researcher notes, which I had been keeping since the start of my dissertation study. In truth, I had begun to document my thoughts as part of the grieving process for my husband, and so I carried the habit over into my research shortly after. My notes revealed repeated phrases of "I am doing this for you, Samuel." "Samuel, I hope you'll be proud of me." And "Things will be better when I have finished the program."

But the reality was that my life had not drastically improved once the words *Dr. Garrison* were put out into the universe. I had falsely placed so much expectation and hope into earning this degree. Like the road ahead was going to be paved in gold-leaf photocopies of my dissertation, with recruiters, millionaires, and government employees lined up on either side with job offers in hand. But as with everything in life worth earning, I still needed to do the legwork. I had to update my résumé, increase my teaching experience, and get more publications under my belt. But that was going to be a logistical challenge because I was a sole parent (one of the preferred terms widows use in lieu of *single parent*) and my kids were not school age. If I took on a job in academia (which was my dream), it would mean inevitably a pay cut of some kind. I simply could not afford childcare and work at a university immediately after graduation.

So I did what any person crazy enough to do a terminal degree would do—I kept working harder and harder and sometimes for a pittance. I landed a fellowship position with my university that allowed me to work part-time and virtually—the only way I would have been able to accept the position. At one point, I was conducting two electronic survey studies, writing a book chapter for an academic volume, and trying to present at a conference. The burnout was fast encroaching, and still there was no increase in pay or happiness. My dad, who watched all of this madness transpire in my home, was unwaveringly supportive (even though I still don't think he knows or understands what it is I actually write about and research). Yet I still felt an emptiness and longing that would not fade away. Why was I depressed?

It was at this point that I presented at a conference in San Antonio with a friend and colleague in my field of research. We had only ever talked or worked together virtually, and so the trip was the first time we had met in person. She was a fast-talking East Coast woman, who was a straight shooter and eager to learn/ grow in her research. We got along straightaway. But she also explained to me that she was a yogi and mindfulness coach. She encouraged me to do yoga or some type of meditation to center myself.

Shortly after the conference, I found a yoga series on YouTube that both my kids and I started doing. After about a month of doing our daily bendies (as I called it to the kids), a realization about my depression hit me like a ton of bricks. I was sad about my degree being over because it was a tangible goal to work toward that distracted me from my widowhood. With it being completed, all of the thoughts lingering in the back of my mind had no homework assignments to address, no papers to write, and so they all flooded right back to me being a widow. I had felt valued and needed as a student in a way that I was now missing as a graduate. And the ways in which I was needed as a widow were beginning to be taxing and mundane.

During the year immediately after graduating, I thought my depression was all to do with my widowhood. I wanted to blame all of my problems with myself and the world on this widowhood thing. By this time, I truly felt that my depression was solely originating from the widow part of my life and had nothing to do with the scholar part of my life. I began to experience another slump/ setback/ backslide/ whatever shrinks du jour prescribe it to be. My depression turned into bitterness, and then I went right back to my default setting: anger.

I was upset that I had not landed a job in academia yet. I was mad that I couldn't pursue opportunities for employment or research because the kids needed me (because it's not like Daddy can watch them). I was frustrated that once again, the universe seemed to put rocks in my life path for no apparent reason.

That is when my dad intervened and provided me with a verbal wake-up call. He validated my feelings, explaining that what had happened to me and the kids (because it was indeed happening to the kids as well) was not my fault or my doing. He told me I was smart and strong and stubborn enough to get through this chapter of our lives. He explained that if a job offer is meant to be, then it will happen. True to dad form, he had prepared a well-structured financial plan to support the many reasons why it may be a good thing I am not working in academia yet (cost of childcare, more quality time with kids in the early years, etc.). He also told me that I have always placed so much pressure on myself to succeed, but that some things in life simply cannot be rushed. He tried to illustrate that even without the widowhood, I would be dissatisfied with myself because it was in my nature to do so.

He was right, of course. I had always been that A-type perfectionista who was so goal oriented that when I didn't have a clear goal, I felt disoriented. That was when I knew my mind-set needed to change to get over this next hurdle in my life and overcome the malaise of postdoc/ postmortem living.

---

Changing one's mind is easy; changing one's mind-set, not so much. I can change which pizza toppings I order with ease, but doing keto and cutting out the crust altogether is something I cannot do (believe me, I have tried). More importantly, there is no clear-cut singular way to change your mind-set. For some, they can switch cold turkey after experiencing a spark of inspiration; for others, it is a long and slow process that must be done incrementally. I am a member of the second group.

After my dad and I had my wake-up call conversation, I did not wake up the next morning all smiles and rainbows. Instead, I made a task list that would help me adjust to my new goal (because, you know, I am in perpetual need of having goals) of changing to a more positive mind-set. I also flooded my life with positive messages and stimuli. In a nutshell, here is how I began to see the glass as half full:

1.  In the United States there are less than 2 percent of the population who have achieved a doctoral level of education. Even being in the middle or bottom of this group is quite an achievement.
2.  I established a personal goal of one publication a year, and began independently contracting trainings and presentations to put on my résumé. I started by reaching out to my children's schools and the local colleges to get my name out there. I joined a young-professionals group in my area. Eventually, the bookings were coming to me without much marketing on my part.

3. I played music that inspired me while cooking, cleaning, and writing. If I did something well, I would buy myself a CD or soundtrack from a favorite film.

4. I saved a bunch of YouTube videos that made me laugh, made me happy-cry, or provoked positive emotions. For me, this included babies laughing and highlight reels or bloopers from my favorite shows.

5. I downloaded numerous TED Talks about grief, happiness, doctoral programs, and motherhood. Some of these talks influenced which direction my research had gone over the past few years.

6. I painted part of a poem in my room ("Phenomenal Woman," by the immortal Maya Angelou). The rest of the poem is written on a bulletin board near my desk. I also enjoy the works of Nikki Giovanni and Dr. Seuss.

7. I continued to do breathing exercises and yoga when I could. I try to commit to at least thirty minutes of activity a day. I have continued to play *taiko* as well and now teach drumming for a group in the Pacific Northwest area.

8. I volunteered in my children's classrooms to watch their faces light up as they learned new skills.

9. I set a goal of learning one new skill a month and going to one new place a month. This varied from trying a new restaurant to learning how to knit, but it forced me out of my complacency, and then I felt pride at doing something new.

10. When I had made noticeable improvement in my mind-set, I took the kids out to celebrate and then set a new goal to continue my progression.

I would like to tell you that I have completed my mind-set shifting and this process is done. But I still have pep talks in the mirror and need reminders to carpe diem. I have been positively reaffirming my existence for almost two years, and there have been many great outcomes from doing so, but every time I snap at the kids or feel like woe is me, I know I need to continue on this path.

I also was wrong about my widowhood being the driver of my depression. After much reflection and speaking to other widows and doctors (of multiple fields), I have learned that many graduates feel sad initially, *and* I have a personality that harkens to negativity versus positivity. It is why I am focused more on mistakes and how to improve them rather than celebrating the little wins in the day-to-day routine.

Understanding this aspect of myself has also had the residual benefit of improving my parenting. Learning to peel back the psychological layers of my life and proactively addressing my needs keeps me more stable, happy, and ultimately more receptive to the needs of my children. Their ability to find happiness in spite of the cards that were dealt to them is amazing. Their resilience to negative thoughts and their coping skills in times of hardship bring tears to my eyes. They are a beacon of light without which I would be lost, widow or not, doctor or not. And this thought helps to drive back the anxiety and motivate me to be all that I can be.

## CHAPTER 9

# Acceptance for Widows

My head out of fog
I finally see myself
In the mirror—oh!

Curative giggles
Come from the kids reminding
That life's still going

There is raw power
In your soul being stripped bare
And still left standing

## I Am a Widow

THERE'S NO ONE MOMENT OF experience or memory that I can recall that made me switch from denying my widowhood to accepting it. It sort of happened in baby steps in very small subtle ways over the period of three years. I can remember filling out paperwork at the dentist office and there being an option: single, married, or widowed. It was the first time I had seen on paper what my status was, and checking that box was a huge step for me in acknowledging to the public that I was in fact a widow. I don't like showing my heartache or burdening other people with my stress and my anxiety and my hurt. So admitting this out loud was a very important step. I also remember just starting to socialize and meet more people who are widows, and it shocked me to see how put together they were trying to be just like I was trying to present myself as being put together. But really they just needed a friend to talk to.

My son enrolled in peewee football in the winter of 2018. At their first practice, I saw this handsome gentleman playing with his son on the field and his little girl running around underfoot. And I was helping keep an eye on her because I know what it's like to have two kids running two different directions. I got to talking to him, and he told me that he, in fact, was a widower. He had just lost his wife twelve months ago to very horrific and fast-acting cancer. The family was still healing from that devastation.

There were a lot of things that happened in that moment. In the span of a second, we had locked eyes and bared our souls and our pain to each other. For me, it felt like dream-fasting that Gelflings do in *The Dark Crystal* movie. I hoped we would we exchanged phone numbers. We did. And to be honest, nothing romantic ever came of it. But there was something heartwarming about meeting somebody who's experienced tragedy at the level you've experienced tragedy. In many respects, we both are dealing with the loss of a spouse in a very unexpected premature way, raising two children on our own boy and a girl each. It was looking to his strength that gave me more strength, looking to his ability to say it out loud to strangers gave me the strength to say it out loud to strangers. That was very important and a huge part of my acceptance.

Eventually, I found the joy and dark humor of widowhood. My grandmother, who had lost our grandpa a few years prior to me, had placed my husband's ashes next to my grandfather's in the family shrine. My grandmother is a total badass. She survived childhood wars, learned two languages, raised six children while my grandpa was away at war, and is a widow. She is my widow superhero. She is also old-school Japanese, meaning that she oscillates from perpetually seeking perfection to acting like a Japanese game show host. Being of Japanese descent, it is traditional in my family to place special keepsakes and tokens on the shrine to honors our relatives. It is also customary, as I found out as a widow, to talk to the ashes every day at 6:30 a.m. When I go to visit my grandmother in her home, I now know to expect a violent wake-up call at zero-dark-thirty from a creaky-voiced ninja saying, "Oi, wake up! Time to talk to husbands at the *hotokesama*."

The most endearing and enjoyable part about this experience is watching my grandmother yell at my grandfather from beyond the grave. He was never hard of hearing in life, but now, my grandma feels it necessary to shout everything to him to make sure he hears it in the heavens. And of course, she dominates the conversation (he never really replies).

But then she instructs me to talk, and I find myself laughing out loud at the spectacle of us kneeling and talking to a few jars in a dresser drawer. I really have nothing to say to Samuel because I talk to him quietly all the time. While I am dreaming, driving, brushing my hair, he forever remains part of my life conversation. So when I am on deck, as it were, to speak to his urn, I simply say the mantra of "love you"/"miss you"/"kids are doing great."

This seems to be enough to pacify the would-be samurai in my life. And just when I think it is safe to go back into the water of normalcy, she throws in a quirky curveball. "Kyupi-chan, you need to place something on his altar."

Great, now what do I put there? He already has a great deal of things that speak to the man he was—a Lego figure from *The Lord of the Rings*, a few art and crafts the kids have made—so what else was symbolic of my husband? Then it hit me. My husband loved food! I daresay it was his first love and I was a close second.

I remember us getting away for a romantic weekend to a resort where they provided chocolate chip cookies to guests upon check-in. I can recall getting to our room, going to bathroom to slip into something more comfortable (wink, wink), walking out, and finding Samuel covered in cookie crumbs and smeared chocolate. His head darted up quickly and said, "Oh sorry, honey, you didn't want any, did you? Here, I will go get some more from the lobby."

He then glided past my negligee-wearing, half-naked self and proceeded to get more cookies. When he returned, he was empty-handed but covered in even more crumbs and chocolate. "Oh, sorry, babe, they were all out and will let us know when there are more."

It then took him another twenty minutes to notice my outfit and that my intentions had nothing to do with eating cookies. But that was Samuel. He lived for his chocolate and was an absent-minded genius to boot. I fell in love with this man-child and love him still for these true Samuel traits.

So when my grandmother asked me what I was going to put in the shrine, I told her I was going to leave Samuel a big slice of chocolate cake. I placed the cake in the shrine and left the room to check on the kids. When I returned, I was met with another ferreted glance from someone covered in chocolate. Only this time, my grandma had scarfed the cake and was covered in crumbs. The plate and fork had been placed neatly back in his spot on the shrine.

Her reaction was priceless. "Oh my god, Zarina-chan! Look! Samuel ate the cake!"

I feigned shock and amazement as I approached her to wipe the crumbs off of her face. She chuckled, the sort of old-lady chuckle that audibly is not so loud but make her whole body shake from the shoulders.

"Okay, Zarina, I tell the truth. When you leave, Samuel told me to eat a cake. He didn't want it to go bad."

And while this excuse was totally the machinations of a sweet-toothed crony, in my heart, also knew that to Samuel, a wasted piece of chocolate cake was sacrilegious. So I smiled and hugged my grandma. "I know," I replied. "That's why he told me to bring the fork with it."

We both hugged again, laughing and embracing, crying and sighing. We were both alone but together; we were both hurting but laughing. It was going to be okay. Everything was going to be okay.

———————————————

It is funny how little time we spend discussing our death with our loved ones. When I married Samuel, the only reason we had started talking about life insurance and our final wishes was for our adoption application. I mean, I am smart, at least smart enough to understand the natural order of life. And on some level, I knew that one of us would outlive the other. But we never dwelled on it much. I am unsure if we did this as a means to deny our fate or simply because we were young and in love. But I don't think we are alone in this. Most people do not have the final conversation. It is painful, scary, and so ultimate. But the reality is that fate did not take Samuel from me to hurt me; fate took Samuel for reasons I do not know, understand, or appreciate.

The lessons I learned from my doctoral program about not taking things personally was reflected in this. I could not take Samuel's death as a personal attack from the universe. I could not fall victim to negative thinking or a negative mind-set. My happiness, my growth, and my future with my kids were all nested in the acceptance of his passing.

There is no litmus test for when you have accepted your spouse's death. But for me, *acceptance* meant that I could admit out loud that I was a widow without feeling insecure or judged. *Acceptance* was not breaking down into tears when describing my life to others. This did not happen overnight. I had to state that I was widowed many, many times before I either got numb to the phrase or could say it matter-of-factly. My social media, website, and biographies for various publications all have updated statuses reflecting my acknowledgment of my status.

But I would caution to people not to wear your widowhood as a badge of sacrifice, but instead as a badge of honor. Do not use your new title to seek sympathy from others. You are better than that. Frankly, sympathy will come at you unexpectedly and unsolicited, and when it does, it will be worth ten more times the weight of compliments and false love you fished for while dropping the widow card on people inappropriately. One of my sisters often reminds me to be an ambassador of widows. She says, "Don't be *that* widow."

Now I proudly state that I am a widow without the expectation of other people getting the feels when I share it with them. It has provided me with unanticipated benefits. When people see you proudly and strongly carrying your identity, they see confidence and drive. I have had so many doors open for me because of my ability to persevere instead of fall victim to circumstance. This characteristic resonates with people. They are drawn to it, and eventually it can eliminate your social isolation or professional stalemate.

But the true winners of acceptance are the children who have lost parents. My kids have learned to accept their situation faster and with far less emotional collateral than I ever could. Sure, there are times where they are triggered. I myself accept the fact that triggers will continue to happen for all of us. But they bounce back so fast. They talk and draw and wear their badges with pride. They like who they are, and if other people judge them for it, they already know it is that person's problem, not theirs. In their own way, they have begun educating people about grief and loss. Sometimes it is through their actions; other times it is through their words.

My daughter and I were at a safety fair for her Scout troop. We were watching a fireman cut open a car to show how they can rescue people. She raised her hand to ask a question but instead stated to the crowd, "My daddy died in a car accident."

Everyone got silent for a second, waiting to see how I would react. The fireman was amazing, and said gently, "Well, I am sorry to hear that."

And then he did something that showed my daughter that what she said was not wrong or inappropriate. He accepted her situation and showed interest in her.

"Did it happen here?" he asked.

She replied, very matter-of-factly, "No."

After that, he knew she was emotionally going to be okay, and the presentation continued. Now had I been embarrassed or insecure, I could have made this scenario a negative experience. I could have yelled at her. I could have rushed away. I could have shamed my daughter for talking about her dad in public. But I resisted. I knew that part of her strength comes from me, and showing her that I have accepted our lives gave her the ability to share it freely with others. Acceptance is not easy, nor is it a task that gets a resounding thank-you. But acceptance can provide you inner peace and outward strength. Moreover, when I dip into the other cycles of grief periodically, my acceptance of Samuel's death has made these cycles less intense and less frequent. Acceptance, my friends, while different for everyone, is the road back to a life worth living.

# CHAPTER 10

# Acceptance for Doctors

## I Am a Doctor

AFTER HEARING MYSELF CALLED DR. Garrison for the first time, I went into a major wave of denial—imposter syndrome all the way. I tried rationalizing that I was just a normal person who was casual and not elitist. "No, don't call me doctor. Call me Zarina," I would tell colleagues and friends.

Or I would joke about my new title, "Well, you have to call me doctor until the student loans are paid off."

But the truth was that I was scared of being judged for being uppity or undeserving of this title. It didn't fit me yet. That is when I started mentoring classmates who had not finished the program. I saw myself in them and also saw how far I had come on my journey. By sharing my experiences and challenges and solutions with my peers, they began to make progress. But without prompting or bribing, they also started calling me Dr. Garrison. They not only appreciated the work I had done to earn this title, but they were also showing me respect for the work I was doing with them.

My dad, ever the military man, said that Dr. Garrison was my new rank. My mother-in-law combined it with my first name and started calling me Doctrina. Gradually, those around me whose opinion mattered to me had accepted my doctoral identity long before I did. When I started hearing it more and more, I gradually began to embrace my new title.

Since I completed my oral defense in August, I had to wait until the springtime to attend commencement and walk in my graduation. And I *so* wanted to walk in my graduation. The wait seems endless, but with each passing week, there were more signs from the universe that I needed to embrace this new chapter in my life. First, my dissertation appeared online in a reputable database. Then, I received a hardcover-bound copy of it in the mail. My degree also arrived in the post the same day that a relative had purchased and engraved a present with the inscription "Dr. Garrison."

My father purchased my tam and gown for graduation as a gift; it was even custom-tailored to my five-foot-nothing body. As the big day approached, I had been increasingly willing to refer to myself as Dr. Garrison. When I walked across the stage and shook the hand of my dean and was hooded by one of my mentors, my heart could have burst from my chest. I do not typically get proud of myself, but that day, I was proud—proud to have survived the journey, proud that I didn't let losing Samuel stop this goal from being achieved, proud that I have provided an example to my kids that speaks to the endless pursuit of knowledge (whatever that will look like for them).

Walking in the doctoral procession after the ceremony, I saw friends and family who had come out to cheer me on. They were even nice enough to throw me a party at my aunt and uncle's home.

It had been such a long time since the family had all gotten together for me. Not to say that they never have done anything for me. We are simply too large and too spread out to get together for family gatherings the way we used to in my youth. In fact, it was the bitter humor in me that noted at Samuel's funeral how nice it was to have the family all together again. But that was three years ago. Between the funeral and my graduation day, I had not spent any time with my family, my one true pillar of strength. This was partially because I was depressed and isolating and partly because I geographically was distanced from many of my relatives and did not have the money to travel.

But whether it be to the adrenaline high of finishing my degree or my ability to find pockets of happiness again, I made the journey to my university for the graduation. I am incredibly thankful I did not just for the chance to spend time with loved ones but also for the chance to begin networking with fellow doctors, who in my mind, were the final hurdle to gaining self-acceptance as a doctor like a rogue chimpanzee currying favor to be inducted into a neighboring colony. I know we should teach people not to rely on the acceptance of others to feel fulfilled. But I wanted it nonetheless. I needed the validation from not just friends and family but also from others who have walked the same journey as I did.

When I was at that conference in San Antonio presenting with my colleague, she introduced us at the beginning of our presentation. She also shared that this would be the first presentation I have given with the title of Dr. Garrison. This prompted the entire lecture room to fill with applause. I could not believe that a room full or experts, scholars, and doctors were all clapping for me. The feeling was surreal.

Later that evening at the conference dinner, I was awestruck yet again when two professors (experts in their field) approached me to discuss my research. These individuals were literally writing the textbooks that I had to read to graduate, and here they were, chatting with me over cocktail weenies! The feeling was unbelievable.

Toward the end of the conference, many new friends and I exchanged contact information. It occurred to me that the pedestal I had placed these people on the week prior was not there anymore. Here I was amongst peers who all ran the doctoral gauntlet like me, and all came out the other end willing to help and support a new member of their ranks.

---

Acceptance of earning a doctoral degree, like accepting widowhood, looks different for everybody. I needed repetitive, positive, and subtle reassurances that I had indeed completed my degree and could legitimately be called doctor. For others, there may be a parade the day they successfully defend their work. If you are like me and going through major imposter syndrome or if you simply need the friendly reminders, write it on your bathroom mirror with a dry erase marker. Say a positive mantra to yourself about you accepting your newfound title. Harken back to the time before your program and remember what motivated you to enroll in the first place. For me, becoming a doctor was important for many reasons. So while it was true that after graduation, I did not have my dream job (yet) or a million dollars (not pesos), I did fulfill what I had set out to do.

My degree gave me freedom to work from home and be there for my kids as their sole parent. It has opened doors to opportunities and social groups I never thought possible. I have traveled the world presenting my work to people who not only understand it (sorry, family, I know you tried) but also are keenly interested in it! I didn't reinvent the wheel, nor will I go down in history for my work, but I have established environment of learning and goal achieving for my kids. Who knows where their journeys may lead? Perhaps we will be a whole family of doctors? Or perhaps I will have taught them through my example to never give up on a dream even in the face of soul-crushing grief? But as sure as I am (and proud to be) a Dr. Widow, I know that they are the living embodiment of Dr. Kiddos. (see what I did there?).

# CHAPTER 11

# The Road Ahead

NO ONE PREDICTS THE FUTURE better than my mother. She not only has accurately predicted the gender of all of her grandchildren (even the adopted ones), *but* she also predicted how our love lives would be as adults. For me, she said that I would marry my one true love. Indeed, Samuel and I had a love for the ages. She also said that she knew I would always become a doctor. This gift was inherited by my grandmother (you remember the chocolate-cake-eating ninja) who could also smell the pregnancy on somebody even before they knew. I, unfortunately, lack any and all otherworldly skills of prediction and premonition. I, like most mortals roaming this earth, can only hope and dream about what is to come. But based on my journey so far as a Dr. Widow, I can tell you honestly that I am excited to dream my dreams and hope my hopes.

## Family Goals

I WANT MY CHILDREN TO continue to heal and grow from this whole ordeal. I am fortunate to have finished school while they are young enough to maybe forget some of Mommy's late-night studying craziness. But the nightmares about Daddy still crop up once in a while, and there will be events (like daddy-daughter dances) further down the road that I know will trigger them in some way. I cannot take their pain away, but I can teach them how to cope in a positive and healthy manner. This life lesson, I hope, is taken to heart because in my experience, I have learned that this is something we need to teach more children (and adults), especially those who are grieving. My kids, like me, will never fully get over losing Daddy, but we have and will continue to find joy in the small things and be happy with the lives we still have to live.

Using what little predictive ability I have, I can see my daughter being a CEO or a head cheerleader one day. My son will become a dinosaur (according to him). But when that dream inevitably fails, Mommy will be there to pick up the pieces of his broken heart and tell him to go into paleontology. I am thankful that they are siblings and that they have each other. More so than I ever could, a sibling can relate the loss of a parent to the other. And while I still find it bleak to think about my own death, it is a great comfort to me knowing that these two will still have each other whenever that day comes (I am aiming for 2085).

But they are also at such a cool age right now (five and six), and beyond the grief, I want them to have the childhood of a lifetime. We are fortunate to have friends and family that nuzzle them in endless love and support. But my kids will also appreciate the sense of adventure and learning new things. My biggest hope for them as they turn eighteen and fly the nest to college and beyond, is for them to think to themselves, "What can I do today?" instead of "Look what I can't do."

It takes time, hard work, and a little bit of luck, but any goal is attainable with the right mind-set. I can picture them showing me pictures of their travels one day with their own families and learning new things that excite and awaken their spirits. Of course, I can also picture them coming home with a tattoo at fifteen, so until they are fully functioning adults, I must remind myself to tether their kite strings just a little bit.

## Career Goals

I still desire to teach in a university. I realize in a day and age when everything is going virtual or adjunct, this dream will be hard to fulfill. But I love talking face-to-face with students about a variety of topics, and it is a bridge to becoming a mentor to them like I was mentored.

After Samuel died, I began to appreciate the gift that is human interaction. Connecting with people has always been something I enjoyed in my work. I can also see myself conducting more research and publishing my findings because my inner geek does a happy dance each time that I do. This includes sharing at conferences and traveling the world with fellow like-minded geeks. Perhaps this will lead to a chance to be a keynote speaker or even present my own TED Talk (hint-hint to any readers out there who knows somebody at TED Talk—Mr. TED would be preferable).

I can easily see myself becoming more prevalent in the widow community. This means becoming a guide and source of support for others walking this journey. My little sister recently lost her husband and found herself in the same situation I was three years ago. I know what you are thinking—what are the damn odds that two sisters both became widows in their thirties? We thought the same thing. She has relied heavily on my lessons learned. I thought it would trigger me or upset me to address her barrage of questions. But the more I helped her, the more at peace I became with certain issues related to my grief. I think the act of helping others is quite therapeutic, and at times like this, why wouldn't you want to pay it forward?

Ultimately, it doesn't matter what I am doing so long as I am able to still provide for my kids. My new positive-mind-set training has taught me to find joy in all things, so if I continue adjunct work or get back into corporate training/ analysis, I will be happy. I just want to provide for my kids the childhoods that Samuel and I had always envisioned. It is a great comfort to know that with my new degree in hand, that road will less bumpy. Oh! And at some point, I want to go on a corporate retreat. No real reason besides the fact that I have never done one, and it is on my bucket list.

There is also a dream I have of running my own *taiko* drumming school. As of now, I have been playing in various groups for over twenty-six years and currently leading a local community group where I live. *Taiko* has truly become one of my life's passions, and I would love to share my heritage, my art, and loud noises with my community. This role would be equal parts teacher and business owner, which is exactly what I am. So again, if you know somebody who knows somebody (angel investors, Bill Gates, J. K. Rowling, for example), you send them my way.

## Travel

Samuel and I had promised to travel the world together someday. While we made it to three continents together, he had to leave a few rest stops early. Now when I go new places, I bring a pinch of his ashes with me and spread them in locations where it is permitted. I used to be sad that we would never have this global adventure together, but now I look forward to trekking our planet with our children. These two kiddos of mine are so full of life and curious that it would be a crime not to share these experiences with them. We are gearing up for our first family trip to visit relatives in London for Christmas. My daughter is already watching and rewatching episodes of *Peppa Pig*. Who knows, maybe my kids will join the Peace Corps one day? But my new travel goal is to visit all seven continents with my children. It will certainly be a long-term goal, but one I look forward to progressing in, one trip at a time.

## Romance

Ah yes, romance—a topic on every widow's mind. Love and romance are two different things. Let me establish that right here right now. And what we define as *romance* varies from person to person. I was never the type of woman who wanted flowers and chocolates. But receiving some sort of attention, especially as of late, would be much appreciated. Walking this world alone is cold and empty at times. There is no one to tell how your day went, no one to have your back always. Some widows seek to replace this loss of companionship with friends, sometimes friends with benefits. Others can find love again whether that be long-term relationships or remarrying. Then there are others, like myself, who are unsure what they are going to do regarding this facet of their lives. In my case, I know that neither Samuel nor I wanted the survivor to be lonely forever. I know in my heart he is okay with me dating and moving on in a sense.

But I also worry about my kids who will forever be the top priority of my life. If I brought someone new into their lives and it didn't work out, how would they feel? Or worse, what if this new person harmed my kids in some way? I would need my dad to raise them while I sat on death row for vehicular manslaughter.

The truth is I would like to meet someone in the future. But they would need to be patient and understanding. Becoming single due to loss is different than divorce. Love doesn't fade away—it just transmutes into something treasured. Some people who have not been widowed do not get this, and they do not share well. My husband and I were also high school sweethearts. There was a lot of time and investment in that relationship, and I knew so much about him and his family before we married. The dating scene to me is both foreign and a bit scary. I suppose I need to channel my feelings toward the universe and let things happen naturally. If it is meant to be and all that.

In the meantime though, it would be nice not to go to a movie by myself or have someone else pick up dinner. As with a lot of things in widowhood, love and romance cannot happen in a vacuum. Putting yourself out there and hanging out socially with others does make this process easier. So I am committing to socialize more and dream of a day when this presents an opportunity for the next great love in my life. Time will tell.

## Personal Goals

While I wander the earth with my littles, I cannot forget the love I need to give to myself. Self-care is critical to surviving any hardship, but especially loss and the trials of higher education. Over the years, I have learned more about myself in the healing process than I ever knew before. My dream for myself is to continue to work on my health, my mind-set, and my happiness. So far, I know this will include playing *taiko* drums, losing weight, and trying to celebrate the little wins as much as the big ones.

Small things like a pedicure or a new haircut to treat myself are nice. But I also recognize that I need to do a mom trip in the near future. A large part of my self-care is also surrounding myself with people that are positive instead of negative. The old adage "misery loves company" is certainly true when going on the dual journey of doctor-widow. And the journey hasn't ended; in fact, in many ways, my journey as Dr. Widow has just begun.

# CHAPTER 12

# Haikus for the Soul

ONE OF THE WEIRDEST PIECES of advice I received about grief was to write my feelings down in the form of a haiku. Short, sweet little blurbs about my pain and joy. I hated doing them at first. By about the fiftieth haiku, I began to realize that breaking down my emotions to the syllable was helping me to break them down in my head. I was better able to dissect and attack the challenges and mental roadblocks I had placed in my mind. So for your viewing pleasure, here are some of my favorites. I keep writing them, but now to motivate me when times get tough. I encourage you to find a mantra, poem, piece of art, or make your own phrase that keeps you moving forward.

*I keep reliving*
*The crash that took you from us*
*Relive; you cannot*


*I woke up last night*
*Seventeen times yet again*
*Widows never rest*


*The kids are growing*
*They both started school today*
*You are missing it*


*Where did my love go?*
*Will I ever be able?*
*How can I manage?*


*Alone now always*
*I lost more than a husband*
*I lost my best friend*


*Life still holds beauty*
*But I feel guilty because*
*It goes on sans you*

*No regrets harbored*
*From the last words we whispered:*
*"I love you, baby."*


*The last time we loved*
*Happened in a dark closet*
*To hide from the kids*


*You favorite, blue*
*So why the fuck did your mom*
*Pick red, which is hers?*


*I'm lost without you*
*I am numb with no senses*
*My soul now wanders*


*The kids are stronger*
*Than me, they are braver too*
*To go on, smiling*


*Our little girl*
*She misses you every day*
*Awake and in dreams*

*Our handsome son*
*So young when you departed*
*Knows your face, not you*


*I spread your ashes*
*In the place we first made out*
*Seventeen years ago*


*Half of my life, yes*
*We were high school sweethearts, yes*
*But life partners, no*


*Who knew that "soulmates"*
*Can sometimes experience*
*What I call soul breaks?*


*Waiting to find you*
*Was two days/ eternity:*
*Fear, hate, deny, sad*


*Today I went pee*
*And the toilet seat was down*
*Some changes are nice*

*I'm a single mom*
*I did everything right, but*
*I'm a single mom*

*After losing a spouse*
*Your phonebook changes, sadly,*
*But you know true friends*

*Shut the hell up please!*
*Is what I want to say to*
*False empathizers*

*I am embittered,*
*I am broken, but I forget*
*They don't understand*

*Two-for-one coupons*
*As useless to me now as*
*Your old gaming gear*

*Penguins mate for life—*
*Thank goodness I'm not penguins;*
*We mate as needed*

*No-shave November*
*Is all year long for widows . . .*
*Silver linings, yay!*

*The loneliest day*
*Was not the day you left me.*
*It was your birthday.*

*Empty my vessel.*
*Hollow is my heart, weak my fight.*
*Hardened is my skin.*

*Loss does not heal clean.*
*It cuts deeper and deeper,*
*Leaving scars behind.*

*Grief is not a phase.*
*It is a state of being.*
*So get used to it.*

*Do not say sorry.*
*Apologies are for those*
*Are wrong, not been wronged.*

*Do you remember?*
*I try to see your smile.*
*Do you remember?*

*We talked about death.*
*You said I could remarry*
*Jason Mamoa . . .*

*You thought about life*
*You thought about afterlife*
*You carried out death*

*We both said our vows,*
*Made promises to remain*
*Broken promises.*

*I always won fights.*
*You said I would outlive you.*
*Way to win this fight . . .*

*Your son just farted,*
*And in a demented way*
*I recall your smell.*

*The tree that you hit*
*Was scorched beyond reckoning*
*Much like my spirit.*


*I miss your cooking:*
*Microwave popcorn and . . . wait . . .*
*I miss my cooking.*


*Kids having bad dreams*
*Crying your name in the night*
*Me, helpless to right*


*Food has no flavor*
*And sleep has no refreshment*
*After losing you.*


*Crying is okay.*
*Hurting means the love was real,*
*And tears are its proof.*


*Just cry it all out*
*Until your face is caked with*
*The salt of heartache*

*People are real dumb.*
*They mean well; but don't get it.*
*Blind yet say "I see."*


*You promised last year:*
*Let's travel the world freely.*
*Your spirit does so*


*Halloween has come*
*And our family costume*
*Is missing a piece*


*The pumpkin patch trip*
*Was lacking your terrible*
*Ill-timed puns and jokes.*


*You loved to pig out.*
*Thanksgiving was no different.*
*Leftovers still here.*


*I learned to make meals*
*Cook your favorite dishes*
*And now you can't eat.*

*Why can't I hear you?*
*That voice in life I silenced—*
*Only now to crave?*


*Shattering silence.*
*When the day is done, it creeps*
*Like a life stop watch.*


*I think I feel it . . .*
*That flicker of life and love . . .*
*Nope, I feel nothing.*


*Will I ever date?*
*Widowed ex-high school sweetheart.*
*Online dating foul.*


*Do you see me there?*
*In the heavens among stars*
*Do you dream of me?*


*My head out of fog*
*I finally see myself*
*In the mirror—oh!*

One, two, three, and four
Each one closer to sleeping
Beer and Lunesta


Heartache and sorrow
Are two synonyms for grief
But they don't come close


When one door closes
They say another one opens,
Where the fuck is it?


Curative giggles
Come from the kids reminding me
That life's still going


So time heals all wounds
But time stopped when you left me
So what happens now?


You deserved to live
You were better in all things
Than myself who remains

*Reconciling*
*My grief with my guilt and calm*
*That you have passed on*


*There is a stillness*
*To the spouse who is living*
*Like a walking death*


*No one can judge me*
*Gummy Bear in hair—don't care*
*I'm a damn widow!*


*You are ignorant.*
*You didn't speak to be cruel,*
*But your words cut deep*


*You came in my dreams*
*To stare but not to engage*
*You fade as I wake*


*Car accident death*
*Tragic, senseless, and sudden*
*No time to prepare*

*The world became gray.*
*Colors, tastes, emotions dulled*
*Perpetual haze*


*Rainbows after storms*
*There is hope that this baggage*
*Will become lighter*


*New first-date jitters*
*Compare apples to oranges*
*Uh-oh, big mistake*


*My very first kiss*
*Was with you while playing golf*
*My last kiss, who knows?*


*I will date again.*
*No one should trek life alone,*
*Nor cope with death too*


*Someday my children*
*Will see the bittersweet strength*
*That Mommy perfected*

*Dreamland is far off*
*I no longer visit it*
*In the sleepless nights*

*I married you knowing*
*Sex would only be with you*
*Until you left; now what?*

*I can't do life solo*
*Then I recall me pre-you*
*I can do life solo*

*There is raw power*
*In your soul being stripped bare*
*And still left standing*

*Today's Thanksgiving*
*Why the hell am I thankful?*
*Oh yeah, for the kids*

*A storyteller,*
*That is what I will become*
*Sharing you with all*

You were born of love,
With endless hopes and wishes
shared by your spirit


We will reunite
In the cosmos as stardust
For eternity


You loved chocolate
Almost more than you loved me
Now it's my linctus


Take some happy pills,
That is what the doctor said
To get over you . . .


Why the fuck should I?
Why should I get over you?
Love is not a switch!


Can you love again?
The heart is able to fit
All new types of love

*My jeans don't fit me.*
*Losing you was a diet.*
*I want my jeans back*


*I am so sorry*
*That every day was not*
*Lived fully with you*


*Primal desires,*
*The fear of being alone,*
*Fading memories*


*Your face was so clear.*
*My mind could recall details,*
*Now it lingers off*


*When we said goodbye*
*We never wanted it to*
*Be the final time*


*Pain is pain is pain*
*It's not a competition;*
*It is brotherhood*

*I am a WIDOW.*
*I am a badass WIDOW.*
*I AM A WIDOW.*


*I am a DOCTOR.*
*I am a badass doctor.*
*I AM A DOCTOR.*


*I, Dr. Widow,*
*Promise to walk both journeys*
*With pride, strength, and love.*

CPSIA information can be obtained
at www.ICGtesting.com
Printed in the USA
LVHW111948030220
645690LV00007B/167/J